St. John's
A BRIEF HISTORY

JOAN RUSTED

WWW.BREAKWATERBOOKS.COM

Breakwater Books is committed to choosing papers and materials for our books that help to protect our environment. To this end, this book is printed on a recycled paper that is certified by the Forest Stewardship Council of Canada.

Library and Archives Canada Cataloguing in Publication
Rusted, Joan, 1946-
St. John's : a brief history / Joan Rusted.
Previously published under title Tolerable good anchorage.
ISBN 978-1-55081-346-3
1. St. John's (N.L.)--History. I. Title.
FC2196.4.R87 2011   971.8'1   C2011-900440-2

  Canada Council for the Arts / Conseil des Arts du Canada   Canada   Newfoundland Labrador

We acknowledge the support of the Canada Council for the Arts which last year invested $1.3 million in the arts in Newfoundland. We acknowledge the Government of Canada through the Canada Book Fund and the Government of Newfoundland and Labrador through the Department of Tourism, Culture and Recreation for our publishing activities.

PRINTED AND BOUND IN CANADA.

To Denis

contents

preface

St. John's is now a thriving, vibrant, modern city — a mixture of the old and the new.

The *National Geographic* Traveler Panel ranked Newfoundland's Avalon Peninsula the number 1 coastal destination in the world in its November-December 2010 issue: "The easternmost point in North America, Avalon Peninsula is home to brightly painted fishing villages and the lively city of St. John's. Judges note its strong social and cultural appeal reflected in music and art, and unspoiled scenery, and they extol its 'stunning natural and cultural integrity.'" Top-rated category destinations are places in excellent shape, relatively unspoiled and likely to remain so.

St. John's: A Brief History aims to give a concise but comprehensive overview of the special place that is St. John's, Newfoundland. The book covers the city's historic background, points of interest, seafaring heritage and marine life, factors that prevented and hindered permanent settlement — or helped it in other instances — the West Country merchants and adventurers who competed for supremacy of the fishery in Newfoundland waters, conflicts between contending groups and laws governing trade between Newfoundland and England, battles between the English and French, our contributions in both world wars, how Confederation with Canada took place, landmarks, historic sites, arts and music, the demise of the cod fishery, the new species fisheries, oil and gas exploration, and the outlook for the future.

Chapter one

NEWFOUNDLAND HISTORY:
FROM FISHERY TO COLONY

War and the cod fishery have shaped Newfoundland's history. Four nations — Spain, Portugal, France and England — each claimed a right to the migratory fishery in Newfoundland waters. England and France recognized the benefit of the fishery as a "nursery for seamen" — a source of trained men for their navies in wartime. Newfoundland's rich fishery and its geographic position at the gateway to North America made it an important region in international diplomacy and balance of power.

The Renaissance brought about many technological changes, making it possible for European ships to explore new lands. John Cabot sailed from Bristol, England, in 1497, landing in North America on the 24th of June, the feast day of St. John the Baptist — from which came the name of St. John's. As no charts or documents of Cabot's voyages exist today, the exact site of his landfall is debatable and is thought to have been either in Newfoundland or Cape Breton, but theories about latitude sailing make the landfall most likely in Newfoundland. In 1583 Sir Humphrey Gilbert arrived with three ships and claimed the colony for England in the name of Queen Elizabeth I.

Western Europe's expansion into the New World began in the 15th century when Spain and Portugal founded colonies in South America for exploitation and financial gain. The fishery brought about a different kind of wealth in the 16th century and the island of Newfoundland became a source of rivalry amongst Spanish, Portuguese, French and English fishermen. The four countries worked out an informal admiralty system to establish order in the harbours, and by 1570 are reputed to have rotated this system amongst the nations. This period has been called the commercial and non-political phase of Newfoundland's history. England's fishery was at first not a national enterprise but was controlled by the merchants of its West Country in southwest coastal England as a private venture for profit. This gave the West Country the key to England's naval strength. Each year, West Country sailors went to the Newfoundland fishery, then to Portugal, Spain and home, gaining valuable seafaring experience in the harsh Atlantic. In contrast, the sailors from London mainly sailed to France and Belgium, not gaining this experience. Soon the British authorities began to see the cod fishery as a basis of naval strength, a means of getting a share of Spanish and Portuguese wealth in markets for fish, and as a way to increase the revenues of the government with tariffs.

THE IMPACT OF WAR

England was involved in 16 wars between the year of the Spanish Armada in 1588 and the end of the Napoleonic Wars in 1815. Many of these wars had an impact upon Newfoundland, and the future of the island hung more upon the result of wars in Europe than on any local battles.

The defeat of the Spanish Armada gave England control of the transatlantic cod fishery. It marked the end of the Spanish fishery but not Spain's power at sea, which was to menace British shipping for many years to come. The decline in the Spanish fishery created a demand for salt fish, which gave England a great opportunity. Only the French and English were left participants in the fishery — as competitors.

The civil wars in England from 1642-1648 were devastating for the Newfoundland fishery, with pirates and Commonwealth cruisers seriously affecting trade and industry. The West Country fishery declined from about 270 vessels during the reign of James I in the early 1600s to about 199 in this later period. Oliver Cromwell's policy was one of protector to Newfoundland, sending ships to protect the fishery. The first real governor of the island was appointed. The governor formerly had been just a manager of a colonization company with no direct commission from the Crown. Newfoundland ships, protected by their escort, traded with Gibraltar, where the fish was later smuggled into Spain and sold.

The Dutch wars followed four years after the Restoration of the Monarchy and dragged on intermittently from 1651-1674. The Dutch were the greatest naval power in Europe at the time. Again, these wars had a direct impact upon Newfoundland. Dutch Admiral De Ruyter raided St. John's, Bay Bulls and Petty Harbour in June 1665, ravaging shipping and shore equipment. Dutch privateers were an aggravation to trade and raided Ferryland in 1673, destroying cattle and burning fishing boats — devastating in terms of manpower, supplies and ship losses. These raids and the worry over the increase in French control on the south coast raised the question of whether Newfoundland should be governed as a settled colony rather than just as a fishing base. This idea was against the West Country merchants' interests because it would mean the loss of their monopoly. As things stood, the merchants controlled the fishery and reaped the profits. Regulations in the Government Charters of 1661 and 1676 concerning Newfoundland stated that it was a naval recruiting ground and discouraged settlement. The English Board of Trade said in 1680, "Newfoundland will always belong to the strongest-sea-power." The island was not self supporting, meaning settlers could not feed themselves or provide the clothing and necessities for survival — all supplies had to come by sea. Newfoundland existed by exporting its fish by ship. Therefore, reality lay in this undisputable fact of possession by the strongest sea-power.

The Fishing Admirals: At this time, Newfoundland was governed by a system known as the "fishing admiralty," which lasted about 150 years. There was no resident year-round governor in Newfoundland before 1729. The captain of the first ship to reach a harbour in the spring was the "admiral" of that harbour for the season and had the first choice of the fishing rooms; the second and third captains became the "vice" and "rear" admirals. The admiral and his assistants were responsible for administering justice. This system was not officially recognized by the British government until 1671. The system did not work well and lawlessness was rampant. Frequent complaints about the state of violence, anarchy and smuggling caused the British government to appoint the first governor with civil authority and the power to appoint magistrates who stayed on the island.

King William's War: The War of the Spanish Succession, known in Newfoundland as King William's War, began in 1689 and lasted until 1697, posing many problems and creating a depression in the fishery. The Spanish and French markets were lost, enemies and pirates damaged the fleets, and navy press gangs brought about a huge reduction in the number of men available for the fishery. England, Holland and Spain were fighting France. France had founded a colony at Placentia in 1662, and in 1696 the French, led by d'Iberville, raided the English colonies, destroying them, committing atrocities and acts of barbarism. In 1697 Newfoundland was in complete ruin and very few records of shipping, settlement and catches were kept during this period. The War of the Spanish Succession ended with the Treaty of Ryswick, and military establishments with a garrison were set up by the British in Newfoundland by 1697, 200 years after its European discovery by Cabot.

Queen Anne's War: Newfoundland's English settlements were attacked on a regular basis by the French from Placentia during Queen Anne's War, 1702-1713. However, there was not much to destroy as the English had not had time to rebuild after the French offensive of 1696-1697. The English wanted no further

French settlement in Newfoundland. English settlers requested help from the foreign office to preserve the colony and protect it from the French.

While war raged on, the fishery had to be carried out or it would never be renewed successfully in peacetime. The fishing merchant faced several problems in wartime. First he had to get fishing ships, men and supplies to Newfoundland, then ensure a safe fishery there, and finally get the fish to market and the ships and men safely back to England at the end of the season. The growth of New England, which at this time still belonged to the English, made it easier to get supplies safely as ships sailed in waters dominated by the English.

The Treaty of Utrecht, marking the end of Queen Anne's War, acknowledged that Newfoundland belonged to Britain. The removal of the French settlers came about only because France had been defeated in land fighting in Europe and its royal and merchant navies destroyed. No further French settlement occurred, but the French were permitted to catch fish and dry them on land from Cape Bonavista to Point Riche. The French fishery was monitored and supervised solely by English control, and this continued until 1783. The French were forbidden to stay during the winter or erect any kind of building, with the exception of the stages and huts needed for the drying of fish. This led to continuous disagreement between English and French fishermen and intermittent problems that have continued to the present time.

The Seven Years War (1756-1763) had a significant impact on trade. The British Empire became much larger, while the French lost their major possessions in North America. Britain's takeover of New France meant that ships from New France traded with England, not with France, and brought more passing shipping trade into Newfoundland waters. Planters and settlers found a greater opportunity to deal with traders and were not as dependent upon the West Country merchants as before. Population in Newfoundland increased after 1763 and there was also an increase in shipping and the amount of American trade to Newfoundland.

It was during this war that Newfoundland was invaded for the last time. The French arrived in Newfoundland and captured Bay Bulls on June 24, 1762. St. John's was difficult to attack by sea, so the French went overland and captured it on June 27. They sent a small detachment to Carbonear and Trinity and these settlements, except for Carbonear Island, were taken as well. St. John's was in the possession of the French from June 27 to September 20, 1762. Colonel Amherst, in charge of New World troops in New York, was notified of the problem and set out for St. John's. He captured Torbay and marched on to Signal Hill where a major battle took place. St. John's was retaken and the French left.

The British fishery began its last big phase of growth from 1763-1770. There was a general expansion in business and an optimistic feeling as the French had been driven out of North America, except for St. Pierre and Miquelon. The French presence had had a dampening influence on English trade in Newfoundland and stymied investment with the threat of war at any time. The whole atmosphere changed after 1763. The fishing ship catch increased from 88,450 quintals in 1759 to 252,910 quintals in 1770. (A quintal, pronounced "kentall," is 112 pounds (50.8 kg), weight for sale, of dried codfish.)

The Treaty of Paris, after the Seven Years War, ceded French possessions in Canada to Britain. Labrador was removed from Quebec and attached to Newfoundland; thus the island's ownership of this vast tract of land originated in 1763, and the title was recognized again in 1927 by His Majesty's Privy Council in England. French fishing rights in Newfoundland were finally verified along "Petit Nord" from Cape Bonavista on the east coast to Pointe Riche on the western shore. The French were brought back to the south coast when the islands of St. Pierre and Miquelon were also given as a shelter for French fishermen on the Grand Banks. Captain James Cook was appointed to do the surveys needed to enforce these international agreements. Cook surveyed St. Pierre and Miquelon in 1763 before they were given to the French, then the French Shore and parts of the Labrador coast were partially surveyed. James Cook's charts were remarkably accurate (many are still used to this day), strengthening Britain's expansion of the fishery into previously unexplored areas and helping the government to curtail French demands for a larger share of the fishery and to keep them within their treaty limits.

While Hugh Palliser was governor, 1764-1768, he charted the south coast near to the French islands and encouraged English settlement in this area. His main concern was to extend English fishing along the coasts and to keep the French within their treaty limits. Palliser made an effort to increase fishing and sealing on the Labrador coast, creating a further demand for ships, fishermen and seamen. The migratory and sedentary fisheries grew and population rose on the island. However, the British government still sought to discourage settlement and to promote the migratory fishery.

England's preoccupation with the French Wars and the temporary restriction on French fishing had given an unanticipated help to settlement, and by the middle of the 18th century more than 2,000 people were living in the area of St. John's. The second Act of Parliament concerning Newfoundland, called Palliser's Act, was passed in 1775. This Act was devised to deter English seamen from abandoning ship in Newfoundland. As stated in a letter in the Colonial Office records, "To controvert the course of nature, to keep the island of Newfoundland a barren waste, to exterminate the inhabitants: to annihilate property, and to make sailors by preventing population." The Act signalled renewed hostility toward settlers, and while it helped the merchants in the fishery they complained of financial hardships imposed upon them by having to guarantee to pay fishermen's wages and take them back to England at the end of the fishing season.

The American War of Independence: During the American War of Independence, 1775-1783, the navy was too busy with defense to pay much attention to settlement, and delayed enforcement of Palliser's Act. The supply routes between America and Newfoundland were cut, causing great but not lasting problems. The colonies in the United States, having gained their independence, were no longer part of the British Empire, and were therefore unable to sell supplies to Newfoundland or the British West Indies. Newfoundland was forced to find other sources of food and lumber, and gradually replaced the American supply links by others in the Canadian Maritimes and Quebec. Newfoundland built its own ships and took over the West Indies fish markets. The migratory fishery had been destroyed during the war and the merchants had to rely more upon the inhabitant fishery, causing a large network of business enterprises to grow up around the Newfoundland coastline.

The Treaty of Versailles, signed in 1783, gave France the islands of St. Pierre and Miquelon to "prevent the quarrels between the two nations of England and France ... take away the fishing rights between Cape Bonavista and Cape St. John and move it to the area between Cape John and Cape Ray on the west coast of the island." This treaty was also to Newfoundland's advantage, as with the loss of their colony at Placentia the French could not attack overland in wartime as they had done previously. The French fishing fleet was working in unfriendly waters, making its fishery very difficult to operate. The French Shore was the cause of endless problems that continued to affect relations between Newfoundland and Britain for many years.

The years from 1783-1789 brought a great post-war boom in settlement — the island's total population increased from about 10,000 to over 16,000 people. The boom collapsed in 1789, but the population did not decline. The Newfoundland population was now too large to remove from the island and could not be discouraged from growing. Numbers had dramatically increased and colonization was a fact. The British government was forced to abandon its policy of discouraging settlement.

War was indisputably the greatest factor, after the fishery, to determine Newfoundland's history. The Spanish and Portuguese fisheries declined because of long, hard wars in Europe which destroyed vast numbers of ships and fishermen. Over the years the fishery was involved in warfare, diplomacy and peace negotiations. If the results of the Seven Years War and the American Revolutionary War had been different, the English position in Newfoundland would have been much weakened and England would not have been able to oppose the demands of the French, Spanish or Americans for the supremacy of fishery and settlement in Newfoundland.

Newfoundland's destiny always had more to do with circumstances in Europe than on the island. Settlement had been held back by the interests of West Country merchants and then the British government's wish to keep the island primarily as a nursery for seamen — not as a colony for settlement. The French defeated the British on the island, but, due to the outcome of the European wars, Newfoundland was ceded to the British with only fishing rights being given to the French. The French lost their Newfoundland colony and suffered a serious loss of ability to compete in the fishery. It was due to preoccupation with the wars in Europe that the British ignored the island for a time, enabling it to become settled to a point that could not be disregarded by Britain any longer — a colony in its own right.

EARLY GOVERNMENT

A resident governor was installed in Newfoundland by 1817 due to the increase in settlement and numbers of people involved in the fishery. Governors began to encourage agriculture, build roads and set up circuit courts.

Newfoundland received official colonial status in the mid-1820s. The settlers continuously pressed for participation in their local government and a representative assembly was granted in 1832. The traditional two house bi-cameral system of colonial government had a Crown-appointed legislature with a fifteen member representative Assembly — elected from nine districts. Difficulties finding a place for the Assembly to sit brought about

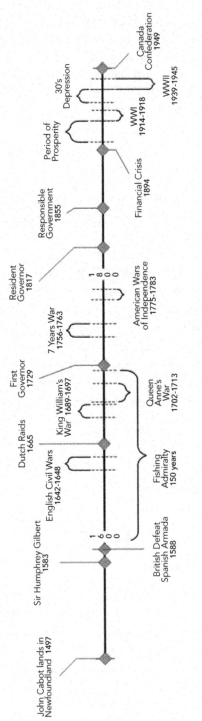

Timeline of events affecting Newfoundland from discovery by John Cabot to Confederation with Canada

DENIS JENKINS

the construction of the Colonial Building, completed in 1850. Tensions between the churches and class divisions played a significant part in the island's political and social life. Demands continued for responsible government.

Newfoundland received responsible government in 1855 and was then equal constitutionally to the other colonies in North America and elsewhere. Much of the money generated by good markets and prices in the fishery during the first years of responsible government was invested back into the island for public improvements and more business establishments. Newfoundland now had control over its economic life, but the economy was based on the fishery. Treaties in place giving privileges to France and the United States to fish, take bait and dry their fish on much of the island's coastline severely limited control of this fishery.

Newfoundland was plagued by many problems in this period when the government was attempting to diversify the economy away from total reliance on the fishery. A devastating cycle of depressions and recoveries occurred with huge amounts of relief given to the people. A movement for confederation with Canada began in the early 1860s but was defeated in 1869 and again in 1894. Railway construction to open up the island began in 1880, was held up by the contractor's business failures, and resumed again in 1890 by the Reid Newfoundland Company. Branch rail lines were constructed to the main towns in Conception, Trinity and Bonavista Bays on the northeast coast, and to the mining industry that had developed in Notre Dame Bay. The dry dock was completed in St. John's in 1884 and brought more employment.

A financial crisis developed in 1894 when runs on Newfoundland's banks, due to reckless investment by officials, forced them to suspend payment. Newfoundland was in a serious position with an economy crippled by the resulting lack of capital and credit. Riots in St. John's ensued from the desperate financial distress of the people. The government of Britain helped with financial assistance and enabled the fishery to start up again.

The years up to 1914 were more prosperous for Newfoundland. In 1898 the government formed a contract with the Reid Newfoundland Company, selling them the railway, St. John's dry dock, contracts for much of the coastal steamer service and the Gulf ferry and telegraph system, centralizing the railway in the west end of St. John's. The Royal Navy Reserve established a branch in St. John's in 1901. The iron ore mine at Bell Island was developed by the Nova Scotia Steel and Coal Company and the Dominion Iron and Steel Company, giving prosperity to the area and employment to hundreds of fishermen in the off season. The pulp and paper industry was introduced in 1905 with the opening of the Anglo Newfoundland Development Company in the Grand Falls area. The town of Grand Falls was built and a rail line constructed to the port of Botwood. A paper mill and the new town of Corner Brook were set up in 1923 — opening the west coast of the island to settlement. These new industries moved employment from complete reliance on the fishery. Newfoundland remained in a recovered atmosphere of activity in the pre-World War I period.

World War I: Newfoundland was a dominion of the British Empire during both world wars as it did not join Confederation with Canada until 1949. World War I was declared on August 28, 1914. The historic **Royal Newfoundland Regiment** was reactivated. The first 500 volunteers were called the "Blue Puttees" due to their distinctive leggings. The regiment fought against the Turks in Gallipoli and against the Germans in France. At the Battle of the Somme and Beaumont Hamel in France in 1916, Newfoundland suffered among the worst losses of any dominion. Nearly 4,000 Newfoundlanders are said to have been killed or wounded. Tommy Ricketts from Middle Arm, White Bay, was awarded the Victoria Cross for bravery, the highest military award given in Britain. Many others served in the British Navy and in the Forestry Corps. Many women served as nurses in Canada, Britain and on the battlefields. At the end of the war the Newfoundland people bought 100 acres of the battlefield at Beaumont Hamel and dedicated it to the memory of the brave men who served in the regiment. A bronze caribou, an exact replica of which stands in Bowring Park in St. John's, overlooks Newfoundland Park at Beaumont Hamel. Memorial University and the War Memorial in St. John's are tributes to the veterans and the war dead. Newfoundland's war effort and contribution caused it to come out of the war with a debt of over $19,000,000.

A British submarine in St. John's harbour, 1915
COURTESY CENTRE FOR NEWFOUNDLAND STUDIES MUN

Commission of Government: The world-wide depression in the 1930s, combined with the huge debt incurred in World War I, brought hard times to Newfoundland. Frustration and un-employment led rioting crowds to attack the Assembly in 1932. The financial position became critical and Britain took over responsibility for Newfoundland's debts with the appointment of the Commission of Government. The Commission, composed of the governor and six commissioners — three British civil servants and three Newfoundlanders — replaced the legislature in February 1934. The Commission was intended to be temporary, but continued when World War II broke out.

World War II: Newfoundland, located strategically at the eastern edge of North America, was called a "floating fortress in the Atlantic" in World War II, and as a consequence was of enormous importance. Its men served in the British and Canadian forces: 3,419 in the Royal Navy; 3,056 in the Royal Artillery and the Royal Air Force; 600 in the Canadian services; and hundreds in the Merchant Navy. More than 500 women were in the Women's Royal Naval Service, Canadian Women's Army Corps or Women's Auxiliary Air Force. One of the largest airfields in the world was located in Gander in 1939 at the beginning of the war, and Newfoundland was a starting and refueling point on the way to and from Europe.

The sea lanes were kept open for supplies, without which victory might have gone to the other side. Over a thousand merchant ships were lost in 1942. Convoys gathered in St. John's harbour to be escorted by an all Canadian escort group before setting off to Europe. One of these, in 1944, was the largest in history: 167 ships. These convoys faced the threat of mines and torpedoes from the waiting German U-boats patrolling in Newfoundland and Atlantic waters.

Mines were set outside the harbour, but were cleared by mine-sweepers. Torpedoes exploded into the chain boom and metal mesh anti-submarine nets across St. John's Narrows in March 1942, but did no damage. Two loaded iron ore carriers were torpedoed and sunk at Wabana, Bell Island, in Conception Bay. In 1941 Franklin Roosevelt and Winston Churchill signed the famous Atlantic Charter in Placentia Bay near Argentia, which declared, "All men in all lands may live out their lives in freedom from fear and want."

American bases were built in Newfoundland in 1941 under the 1940 Destroyers for Bases deal. The arrival of the Americans brought vast changes to Newfoundland and Labrador and well-paid jobs became available. Newfoundland, prior to WWII, was a society of native-born people. It was a radically different place after people from the U.S., Canada and other places around the world arrived here with the armed forces. Fort Pepperrell became the headquarters of the U.S. Northeast Air Command and one of the NATO bases. St. John's harbour was used by the Royal Navy, the Royal Canadian Navy and the United States Navy.

Canada also established significant military facilities: a naval base, two hospitals, a naval barracks at Buckmaster's Circle, a military barracks at Lester's Field and an airport at Torbay. All these factors brought about virtually full employment, more money in circulation, and prosperity.

CONFEDERATION WITH CANADA

The British government did not want to carry on the Commission of Government indefinitely, and a time for change came in 1945, when Newfoundland was financially self supporting. The debate resumed on a possible return to responsible government. But first the constitutional position had to be settled as there was no established procedure to give Newfoundland back its government in this situation.

The British government set up a National Convention in Newfoundland to examine its financial and economic conditions and make recommendations on the forms of future government to be placed on the referendum ballot. Delegates from every Newfoundland and Labrador district met in the Colonial Building. The Convention recommended on the ballot the two options of either continued Commission of Government or return to responsible government. Canada recognized through its wartime experience the strategic importance of maintaining a foothold in Newfoundland and was also concerned about the continued presence of the Americans on the island. Confederation with Canada was not recommended on the ballot, but the British government decided to include it as a third option in the referendum. Two referenda were held and in the second, on July 22, 1948, Confederation with Canada won with a very close majority of 52%. A seven-man delegation was chosen to debate the terms of union that were signed with Canada on December 11, 1948. Newfoundland became the tenth province of Canada on March 31, 1949.

It was said that Newfoundland joined Confederation "not by bullets but by ballots."

With the introduction of Confederation six Newfoundlanders were appointed to the Canadian Senate, seven federal members of Parliament were elected to go to Ottawa and Joseph Smallwood became the first premier of the province of Newfoundland and Labrador. Confederation brought about social changes in the form of unemployment insurance, old age pensions, government paid medical care and hospitals and increased payments for education.

chapter two

FORTS OF OLD ST. JOHN'S

Historically, fortifications were built in St. John's to provide a safe harbour and refuge from attack for fishermen, rather than for the defense of the town or people; 173 years of British military presence in Newfoundland began in 1697 when the British fortified the port. There were seven active batteries during the 1700s and 1800s. When Newfoundland became a colony, the fortifications were used for the protection of the town, which had become the trading and recreation centre of the island. Fortifications developed as did technology. At first all fortifications were at sea level with the cannons concentrating on the narrowest point of the harbour entrance. Eventually, fortifications were moved to Fort William in the east end of the town, then to Fort Frederick (Frederick's Battery) and later to Fort Townshend on the higher levels.

Fort William was an important part of St. John's for over 200 years. It was built in 1680 to defend against the continuous attacks by pirates and privateers. The British were reluctant to build fortifications in Newfoundland, but the fort was improved in 1771 and again in 1795. It was the principal defense for the town and harbour for most of the 18th century.

The barracks for the imperial garrison stationed at Fort William remained in use until 1871. Fort William then served as a railway station until the new station on Water Street was completed in 1903. The old Newfoundland Hotel was built on the site where the fort once stood. This building has since been torn down and a new hotel built in its place.

Frederick's Battery is located between Fort Amherst and Prosser's Rock in the area near Prosser's Rock small boat basin on the south side of the harbour. A battery was established in 1665 after the Dutch Admiral De Ruyter attacked the city. This was rebuilt in 1776 and named Frederick's Battery. A pile of rocks from the old fortifications can be seen and many artifacts have been found on the site.

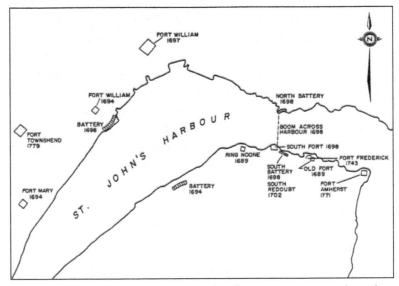

Three centuries of St. John's harbour fortifications concentrated on the narrowest part of the channel. Booms, chains, and in the 1940s, submarine nets between Chain Rock and Anchor Point, required manning and defense.

COURTESY GERALD PENNEY RARE BOOKS AND MAPS OF NEWFOUNDLAND AND LABRADOR

Fort Townshend: This large fortification was built in 1779 to house the military. Its location just west of the Basilica of St. John the Baptist was a better site from which to view the harbour and to fire upon whoever was in control of Signal Hill than was Fort William. The military withdrew from St. John's in 1870 and most of the fortifications were leveled and allowed to fall into disrepair. The former site of Fort Townshend is the present location of The Rooms.

Fort Amherst: Located on the opposite side of the Narrows from Signal Hill, Fort Amherst held a defensive position for over 400 years. In 1762 the British tried to stop invasions of St. John's by extending a chain from Chain Rock to Pancake Rock, and in 1777 constructed the fort. A stone lighthouse was built on the site in 1813. All has now fallen into ruin. The fort was reactivated for defense in both world wars. In World War II a submarine net was placed between Chain and Pancake Rocks to prevent attacks against the harbour by German U-boats, often seen outside the harbour entrance. The fortifications and guns can still be seen at Fort Amherst, as well as a small new lighthouse and foghorn constructed in 1954 to aid navigation.

South Castle Battery: Throughout the history of St. John's harbour, Chain Rock on the east side and Anchor Point on the west side of the Narrows were heavily fortified. These batteries worked with Fort William to defend the harbour. The site of South Castle is fenced off near Prosser's Rock small boat basin. Gerald Penney, an archaeologist, investigated the site in 1988 as part of an environmental study on the Prosser's Rock small boat basin. He said that South Castle was called a "pretty little castle all of stone and substantial timber" by contemporary observer Reverend John Jackson in 1706, and that castle was a common English term for seacoast defenses which contained a tower or "keep." The battery was called South Battery and South Redoubt by its builder, Captain Michael Richards. The substantial eight-gun battery and ancillary fort was built at Anchor Point between 1700 and 1703. It withstood French takeover in the winter of 1703 for 33 days but was taken by land and destroyed by

St. Ovide in January 1709. The battery was believed to be 120 ft (37 m) long and about 15 ft (4.6 m) high. It may have had a wooden sentry and signalling tower, a guardhouse and a powder magazine. The effect of the design was to provide fire, like a ship's broadside, to attack an enemy ship attempting to enter the harbour. The battery may have replaced an even older earthworks battery right on top of Anchor Point. More than 5,000 glass, ceramic and metal artifacts were recovered in 1988 and are held at the Provincial Museum in The Rooms. The derrick pad for World War II submarine nets was excavated at the South Castle dig.

Fort Waldegrave (North Castle Battery): Constructed in 1798 as a temporary battery on the site of the old North Castle Battery above Chain Rock, Fort Waldegrave was used until the 1860s. The battery was reused during World War I with gun

St. John's harbour from Fort Amherst, circa 1886

placements constructed to protect the Narrows. The gun area is presently a parking lot overlooking the Narrows and the placements can still be seen.

Queen's Battery: For centuries France and England vied for possession of St. John's and in 1762 British and French forces fought the last North American battle of the Seven Years War on the slopes of Signal Hill. The fortifications date from the 1840s and 1850s. The barracks and the gun placements have been re-constructed at the original site on Signal Hill below Cabot Tower. **The Signal Hill Tattoo**, a reenactment of the garrison life and duties of His Majesty's Royal Newfoundland Regiment of Foot and the 27th Company 2nd Battalion-Royal Regiment of Artillery, in authentic period uniform, of the late 1790s, can be seen and heard near the Queen's Battery each day during July and August.

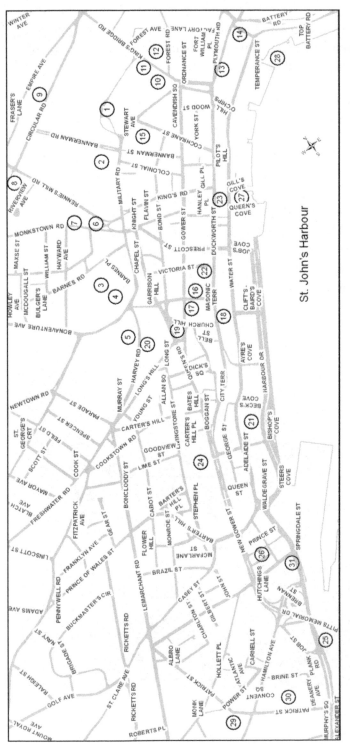

Old St. John's – The Downtown Core
CITY OF ST. JOHN'S

Cuckold's Cove: Batteries were set up at Cuckold's Cove and Quidi Vidi to prevent enemy landings that might take the town from these positions. Legend has it that Cuckold's Cove got its name from a duel fought there between two officers of the old garrison on Signal Hill. It was said that one officer accused the other of paying undue attention to his wife. So, the "cuckolded" officer challenged the other to a duel. Unfortunately, however, it seems that in this case justice did not triumph — the aggrieved party was killed and his fellow officer proceeded to marry the widow.

Quidi Vidi: The narrow entrance to Quidi Vidi, known as the Gut, is a short distance along the shoreline from Cuckold's Cove. **Quidi Vidi Village** is a small picturesque fishing village, with old houses, wharves and small boats. Above the entrance to the small harbour is the **Quidi Vidi Battery,** a reconstructed French fortification from the French capture of St. John's in 1762. The British rebuilt and occupied the fort in 1780 until the garrison left Newfoundland in 1870. The battery was restored as a centennial project in 1967 from old plans and archaeological data. Guides dressed in period costume provide tours showing how soldiers and their families lived on this remote site. The battery has been designated a Provincial Historic Site. **Quidi Vidi Brewery,** a microbrewery offering offseason tours, is located in Quidi Vidi Village.

Fort Pepperrell (Pleasantville): A United States military base was located between Quidi Vidi Lake and the White Hills. The U.S. was granted land in 1941 on a free 99-year lease to construct naval and air bases for the eventuality of attack by Germany. The construction brought millions of dollars into the local economy — an enormous boost after the depression years. Newfoundland entered a period of unprecedented prosperity. The coming of the Cold War meant the building of early warning radar sites in northern Labrador and the continued presence of the Americans. It is estimated that during these years 25,000 Newfoundland women married U.S. personnel. The Americans also built the first modern pier in the port. This pier was in use until 1961 when it was taken over by the National Harbours Board of Canada. The U.S. moved out of Newfoundland in 1966 and turned the Fort Pepperrell base, now known as Pleasantville, back to the province. The base hospital was reopened as the Dr. Charles A. Janeway Hospital for Sick Children, now moved to the Health Sciences Complex on Prince Philip Drive. The Canadian Military, Canadian Forces Base Pleasantville is located on part of the former U.S. base.

A concrete monument was erected, and dedicated in August 1991, on the former Pepperrell Air Force Base property on the north bank of Quidi Vidi Lake. It is the original monument constructed by the United States Marines after they landed at Argentia Naval Station, Placentia Bay, on January 25, 1941, and where the first American flag was raised on Newfoundland soil on February 13, 1941. The flags of the United States, Canada and Newfoundland fly continuously behind the monument.

chapter three

LANDMARKS AND
HISTORIC SITES OF ST. JOHN'S

St. John's has had a long and colourful history as the oldest port city in North America. The entrance into St. John's harbour consists of a narrow gap leading into a deep bay. Because of its harbour and proximity to the fishing grounds, St. John's became a commercial trading outpost for the Basques, French, Spanish, Portuguese and English engaged in the fishery. The harbour was used as a meeting place for fishermen, with Portuguese and Spanish trawlers frequent visitors, from about 1627 until more recent years. The city grew around its perfectly landlocked harbour — a haven from storms.

Only in the 19th century did St. John's take on the appearance of a town. In 1810 it consisted of one narrow street with batteries and fortifications on the higher area of the town. Today the thriving capital city of Newfoundland and Labrador has spread to the north and west of the original town up to the neighbouring City of Mount Pearl, Town of Paradise and Town of Conception Bay South. The city expanded its boundaries in 1992 to include Wedgewood Park and the Goulds. The 2006 census in the metropolitan St. John's area gave it a population of 181,113.

St. John's was a centre of Newfoundland life and commerce, with shipping connections to the U.S., Britain and Canada. It was a place for the distribution of goods and a base for the fishing fleets. It served as a naval base in the War of 1812 and in the two world wars. Today, many buildings and historic sites stand as landmarks and give testimony to the rich history of St. John's and its harbour.

The very fabric and structure of St. John's reflects its political history. Many of its streets are named after former governors — Gower, Prescott, Bannerman, Cochrane — or other people significant in the city's history. Growth of the town was slow until the 19th century when big houses and urban wealth in the town core around the Colonial Building and Government House reflected its importance as an economic, administrative, religious and educational centre of the island.

There was no town council until 1888. Most of the best land was owned by absentee landlords who strongly opposed municipal taxation. The government held the reins of most of the institutions and services of St. John's until that time.

Railway centralization in the west end of the town at the end of the 19th century reinforced the city's importance as an economic centre. The town boundaries had been inside the old track on Empire Avenue until the 1940s. Town planning began during the time of the Commission of Government with the formation of the St. John's Housing Corporation in 1944 and new planned suburbs. The town began to spread from its urban downtown core to the north and west into the towns of Mount Pearl, Paradise and Conception Bay South.

Confederation with Canada brought federal funding for buildings such as the Sir Humphrey Gilbert Building on Duckworth Street, the post office on Water Street and also the St. John's harbour redevelopment. Hotel Newfoundland and the Newfoundland Dockyard were taken over by Canadian National, a government Crown corporation. Premier Joseph Smallwood built a new Confederation Building on Prince Philip Drive for the provincial legislature and government offices, and Memorial University built a new larger campus on Elizabeth Avenue.

St. John's and the Northeast Avalon Peninsula
COURTESY CITY OF ST. JOHN'S ENGINEERING DEPARTMENT

ST. JOHN'S FIRES

St. John's had three major fires in the 1800s: 1816, 1846 and the devastating 1892 fire. Most houses in St. John's were built entirely of wood and were irregularly huddled together. Over 11,000 people were left homeless in the 1892 fire with 1,572 houses burnt to the ground. All that was left standing in most of the downtown area were chimneys and the great empty walls of churches and larger stone buildings. Most of the downtown within the area of Cookstown Road, Carter's Hill and Beck's Cove in the west and Harvey Road and Military Road in the north burned in the fire. The property damage was estimated at $20,000,000 with less than $5,000,000 covered by insurance. Most of the main shops, warehouses and business and professional areas were completely gutted by fire, and the main public buildings, the hospital, the Anglican Cathedral and many churches also lay in ruins. Temporary housing for the homeless was made in Bannerman Park, Quidi Vidi Lake and other open spaces. The town was rebuilt and recovered with the help of many supporters and benefactors.

St. John's after the Great Fire of 1892
E1-25 COURTESY OF THE ROOMS, PROVINCIAL ARCHIVES DIVISION

Each of these fires brought about improvements and changes. Streets such as Water Street were straightened and widened, there were new layouts, rebuilding, and firebreaks made, some of which have become well known streets today. The Roman Catholic Basilica and Anglican churches were built in this period. St. Andrew's Presbyterian Church, the Congregational Church and new Colonial Building were also completed. The fires had an influence on building materials and merchants began to build in brick or stone.

Another devastating fire occurred in December of 1942 when the Knights of Columbus Hostel on Harvey Road caught fire during a Saturday night dance for servicemen: 99 people were killed and 107 injured. There are theories that the fire may have been the result of enemy sabotage. Ironically, another major fire hit the same spot exactly 50 years later in December 1992. The CLB Armory and the area on LeMarchant Road and Long's Hill were gutted, but no lives were lost in the 1992 fire. High winds and intense heat almost caused the fire to become out of control.

DOWNTOWN ST. JOHN'S

The main downtown street, Water Street, was, in the city's early days, nothing more than a row of fish flakes. It was called the Lower Path, and quickly developed to become the centre of city life and commerce. The premises of all the merchants were located along its length. The names of Bowring, Ayre, Macpherson, Knowling, Devine, Newman, Milley, Wood, Outerbridge, Harvey, Murray, Job, Martin, Royal, Hutton, Steers, Hickman, Pratt, Clouston, Dicks and many others were prominent in the town's trade and business. Most of the stores had several wharves, also known as finger piers, jutting out into the harbour, and fish stores or warehouses built on the north side of the harbour. The street was once paved with cobblestones while the other streets were hard-packed dirt.

Water Street, St. John's, circa 1886
CITY OF ST. JOHN'S ARCHIVES

Street cars on tracks were once a familiar sight in the downtown area, running along Water Street, Duckworth Street, past the Newfoundland Hotel, up Military Road to Rawlins Cross, down Queen's Road to Adelaide Street and back to Water Street. The street cars ran from the turn of the century until they were replaced by buses in 1948.

Street car and horse drawn buggy
CITY OF ST. JOHN'S ARCHIVES

Duckworth Street was called the Upper Path when there were only two major roadways in St. John's. Now a busy commercial centre, one of the oldest streets in the city has had many homes converted to offices, delightful shops and restaurants — a blend of traditional and contemporary businesses. Its heritage can be seen in the many historic buildings along its length.

Water Street has undergone significant changes over the years as a result of fire and reconstruction, and new heritage by-laws have been enacted to guarantee that old buildings of character will no longer be destroyed. The exteriors of many are being restored and the interiors modified for contemporary use. Yellowbelly Corner at Water Street and Beck's Cove is but one example of the past style of building on this historic street. Today the old brick and stone buildings still give the street an Old World charm. Water Street is the heart of downtown with its old buildings, shops, boutiques, craft shops, restaurants, coffee shops, and the harbour front. You can enjoy a leisurely stroll along its length and also enjoy the sights and sounds of the harbour.

St. John's Waterfront is a popular place for both visitors and residents to drive and walk, to see and hear the activity of the many ships in for supplies, repairs or to deliver cargo. Cruise liners tower over the buildings when they visit during the summer months.

Today, St. John's has the most pubs per capita in Canada, many of them located on George Street. One can walk up and down its length, dropping into the numerous restaurants, night clubs and taverns, enjoying the atmosphere and considerable choice of music. There is something for everybody: blues, jazz, western, alternative, rock, contemporary or traditional Newfoundland music. Thousands are drawn to the open-air concerts, festivals and social events in the summertime. George Street is one of the main attractions of the city.

Areas of the town are locally known as the East End, West End, Higher Levels, Cookstown, Residential Centre, Downtown, Churchill Park, Georgetown, Rabbittown, The Battery, Pleasantville, Mundy Pond, Cowan Heights, Waterford Valley and Shea Heights.

Quaint fishing villages such as Quidi Vidi, Torbay, Flat Rock, Pouch Cove and Petty Harbour, plus dramatic coastal scenery, can be viewed within a half hour drive of St. John's. Cruising in and out of the Narrows on a boat tour is an experience not to be forgotten. The view of the city is spectacular from the south side of the harbour.

Cruise ship in harbour in 2010
RUSTED COLLECTION

ARCHITECTURE AND HISTORIC BUILDINGS

ARCHITECTURE

St. John's is a city with fine architecture and many brightly painted wooden houses and row housing. Despite destruction wrought by the fires, many buildings standing today reveal its past and are preserved by strict Heritage by-laws.

The Rennie's Mill Road, Circular Road and King's Bridge Road areas contain most of the significant private residences in St. John's. Built by many wealthy merchants, politicians and lawyers in the 1800s, they are excellent illustrations of residential streetscapes in this period. The exclusiveness of the neighbourhood north of Military Road came from its proximity to Government House and the Colonial Building. Many of these large residences have been converted to exclusive Heritage Inns and Bed and Breakfast establishments.

The areas bounded by Military Road, Cavendish Square, Gower Street, Duckworth Street, Bates Hill and Carter's Hill contain many interesting and colourful houses and row houses with steep streets leading down to the harbour. Rows of brightly coloured houses in these areas are known as Jelly Bean Row.

Southcott Style of Architecture — Second Empire: The firm of J. and J. T. Southcott is said to have come from England in the mid 1800s to build houses for the Cable Company in Heart's Content. J. T. Southcott, the first trained architect in Newfoundland, introduced the mansard roof to St. John's. The Southcott style is Second Empire, typified by a concave-shaped mansard roof with rounded bonnet-shaped dormer windows, bracketed eaves, and bay windows on the ground floor — built mainly in the period from 1870 to 1900. The Southcott style became the most representative of St. John's architecture during the time when most of the city had to be rebuilt after the 1892 fire.

J. T. Southcott's home (Monkstown Road) was at one time operated as a hospital by Mary Southcott.
RUSTED COLLECTION

J. T. Southcott's own house on Monkstown Road, built in 1875, survived the 1892 fire and typifies this type of design. Southcott's daughter Mary later lived in this house and in 1918 operated a small private hospital there for maternity, women and children. The house was later sold to the Knights of Columbus and is now a private home. Other fine examples of the original Southcott style can be seen on Monkstown Road, Park Place and Rennie's Mill Road.

Among the distinctive architecture of downtown St. John's houses are the five houses located on **Devon Row**, near Hotel Newfoundland, which also survived the fire of 1892. They were constructed by James J. Southcott in the Second Empire Style in about 1870-1877.

Samuel Garrett Houses: The stone mason who built Cabot Tower also built a row of four Second Empire stone houses for his four daughters on 31-37 Temperance Street east of Devon Row on Duckworth Street. The houses were built entirely of unused stone from Cabot Tower during the times when the weather was too bad to work on the top of Signal Hill. The houses are four storeys high at the back and three at the front. The houses were designated Registered Heritage Structures in October 1988.

Queen Anne Style houses are usually imposing in size, using many roof forms and details, such as decorative shingling and applications from other styles. This style of house was built during the period 1905-1915.

Several fine examples of the Queen Anne style are:

Winterholme, located on the corner of Rennie's Mill and Circular Roads, a National Historic Site, was designated a Registered Heritage Structure in December 1986 and awarded the Southcott Award for heritage restoration in 1996 by the Newfoundland Historic Trust.

The Ryan Mansion, located on the corner or Monkstown and Rennie's Mill Road, was built between 1909 and 1911. It was designated a Registered Heritage Structure in 2001.

Bartra on Circular Road is one of the largest single family houses in the city. Its exterior has remained unchanged since construction in 1905. It was awarded the Southcott Award for restoration in 2002 and recognized as a National Heritage Structure in 1994.

Bryn Mawr, located across from the corner of New Cove Road and Portugal Cove Road, is a large Queen Anne country house.

Many more examples of the Queen Anne style are seen on Rennie's Mill Road, Circular Road and King's Bridge Road.

Victorian Gothic Style: Victorian Gothic or Gothic Revival is represented by a saddle-roofed building with a steep pitch, decorated with Gothic revival details and built during the period 1840-1900. The best examples of the ecclesiastical style in St. John's are the Cathedral of St. John the Baptist and St. Patrick's Church. A fine example of a Gothic Revival great house is Sutherland, built between 1883 and 1885 on King's Bridge Road.

Romanesque Revival Style: The Court House and the Basilica of St. John the Baptist in St. John's are fine examples of Romanesque Revival. Gower Street United Church and Cochrane Street United Church were built in a modified Romanesque style.

Italianate Neo-Classical Style: The former Bank of British North America, a fine example of Italianate Neo-Classical Renaissance style, was designated a National Historic Site in 1990. The Colonial Building was also built in Neo-Classical style.

Bracketed Style: A common form of architecture used in St. John's, the bracketed style, is comprised of a flat-roofed building with brackets placed under the eaves of the roof. Many houses of this style can be seen on Military Road and on the streets leading down to the harbour.

Classical Commercial Vernacular Style: Yellowbelly Corner, the area at Beck's Cove, Water Street, was a meeting place for Irishmen from Wexford, who wore yellow sashes or badges. It was given the Southcott Award for restoration in 2009. The brick and stone building is Classical Commercial Vernacular constructed about 1840–1860 and a type commonly built for commercial use in the areas around Water Street in this period.

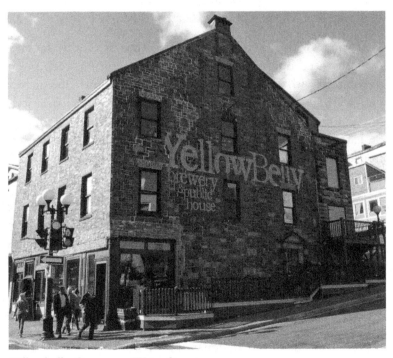

Yellowbelly Corner on Water Street
RUSTED COLLECTION

HERITAGE AWARDS AND DESIGNATIONS

The Southcott Award was introduced by the Newfoundland Historic Trust in 1984 "to recognize excellence in the preservation of the architectural heritage of Newfoundland and Labrador."

The Heritage Foundation of Newfoundland and Labrador:
The foundation was established by the Government of Newfoundland and Labrador in 1985 "to stimulate an understanding and appreciation of Newfoundland's architectural heritage." Each year significant buildings are designated Registered Heritage Structures.

National Historic Site: The Government of Canada through Parks Canada designates National Historic Sites as being "places of profound importance to Canada." Cabot Tower and Cape Spear are National Historic Sites run by Parks Canada.

The Government of Canada also designates buildings of National Historic Significance of Canada. Those in St. John's include Government House, the Basilica, the Murray Premises, the Anglican Cathedral, the Court House, St. Patrick's Roman Catholic Church, St. Thomas' Church, Commissariat House, Christ Church Quidi Vidi, Winterholme and the former Bank of British North America.

Provincial Historic Site: The two designated sites in St. John's are Commissariat House and Quidi Vidi Battery.

Plaques are displayed on each of the buildings showing its award or designation.

The Manning Award: Started in 1993, the award is given by the Historic Sites Association of Newfoundland and Labrador for "Excellence in the Public Presentation of Historic Places to recognize community heritage projects and the work of heritage champions." In St. John's the award has been given to the Basilica Museum, Lillian Stevenson Medical Archives, Railway Coastal Museum and the Newman Wine Vaults.

HISTORIC BUILDINGS

The Roman Basilica of St. John the Baptist: The Basilica, located on Military Road, was designed by John Jones of Ireland in the Romanesque style. It was built of limestone and granite in the form of a Latin cross with two 42 m (138 ft) high twin towers at the front. The sandstone was quarried in Kelly's Island, Conception Bay, the limestone came from Ireland, and Dublin granite was used to face the windows and quoins. The building took 14 years to complete and was consecrated in 1855. It was begun by Bishop Fleming who wanted to build a symbol of the Catholic Church and its importance in the social, economic and political life of St. John's. At the time of its completion the Roman Catholic Cathedral of St. John the Baptist was the largest church in the north of the New World. It was the only principal church in the city to survive the 1892 fire undamaged.

The church was raised to the rank of minor Basilica in 1955 on its centenary. At that time, several thousand Portuguese fishermen paraded to the church to donate the statue of Our Lady of Fatima. The event celebrated the special relationship that had long existed between Newfoundland and the Portuguese fishermen who for many years came to St. John's harbour with the famous "White Fleet."

The Basilica has been designated a National Historic Site. It is one of the best known landmarks of the city and affords an excellent view of the harbour and downtown area from its front steps. It has some excellent statuary and a beautiful intricately painted ceiling highlighted in gold leaf. Its Casavant Freres pipe organ has 4,050 pipes. **The Basilica Archives** holds historical and contemporary documents of the Roman Catholic Church in Newfoundland, including Papers of the Bishops from 1755-1979, as well as baptism, marriage, and death records from 1784-1905. **The Basilica Museum** was originally built in 1859 as a public library and reading room and features 14 panels that tell the story of the development of Roman Catholicism in Newfoundland. It also holds the largest collection in Canada of artistic and historically significant church artefacts that date from 1524, including sacred vessels, furniture, liturgical garb, paintings and books.

The Basilica of St. John the Baptist
RUSTED COLLECTION

The **Presentation Sisters' Motherhouse** in Cathedral Square is now open to the public for tours. The tour includes the masterpiece bust sculpture *Veiled Virgin*. This was hand carved by Giovanni Strazza of Milan from solid Carrara marble and imported to Newfoundland in 1856 from Rome. A Carrara marble altar can be found in the former chapel, as well as a working Regina music box and frescoed ceilings in the former chapel and drawing room by Pindikowski — the same Polish prisoner who painted the ceilings in the Colonial Building and Government House. Pindikowski also painted the ceiling in the Basilica Museum.

The **Anglican Cathedral** is the oldest Anglican parish church in North America. Construction of the present church began in 1847, of white sandstone from Scotland and bluestone quarried in the Southside Hills. The Cathedral is said to be the finest example of ecclesiastical Neo-Gothic architecture in North America, and was designed by Sir George Gilbert Scott. The nave functioned as the church until the transepts and Choir were completed in 1885. The design is of a Latin cross with characteristic Gothic discordant parts and asymmetry of carving, stonework and design. The 150 ft (46 m) spire in Scott's plans was not built as the cost was prohibitive. The Cathedral was given an official coat of arms when it became elevated to Diocese status in 1839. Newfoundland now has three Anglican Dioceses, with the Cathedral representing Eastern Newfoundland and Labrador.

The Cathedral was destroyed in the fire of 1892 and left a shell. The interior was rebuilt within the remaining exterior walls a few years later. The nave and aisles are excellent examples of Gothic Revival. Many magnificent carvings, gargoyles, stained glass windows — one of which escaped the fire — a reredos (ornamental screen of carved white free-stone behind the altar) designed by Giles Gilbert Scot and beautifully designed woodwork and medieval carvings can be found inside this

Watercolour of Anglican Cathedral
COURTESY OF CYNTHIA I. NOEL

Cathedral on Church Hill. The magnificent pipe organ was rebuilt by Casavant Freres of Quebec in 1927. The **Lady Chapel** was refurbished in September 1972, and the **Crypt** restored and opened in 1979. Afternoon tea can be enjoyed in the Cathedral Crypt during the summer months. A small archival museum is open to the public during guided tours.

The area behind the church includes a cemetery with about 5,000 graves. This was founded in 1699, making it the oldest in Canada.

The Anglican Cathedral was designated a National Historic Site on June 19, 1981, given the Southcott award in 1984 and designated a Registered Heritage Structure in 1991. It is a must for those interested in church architecture.

A **Haunted Hike** departs from the steps of the Cathedral at 9:30 pm throughout the summer months. Experience dark back lanes and spine chilling stories.

St. Andrew's Presbyterian Church: "The Kirk" is constructed of Accrington brick and finished in Scottish free-stone with an impressive spire and one of the world's best collections of Balantine stained glass windows. It is said to be one of the finest examples of High Victorian Gothic serence architecture amongst the city's churches and is located on the corner of Long's Hill and Queen's Road. It was built in 1894 after the original Presbyterian Church was destroyed in the fire of 1892. The Kirk was designated a Registered Heritage Structure on October 31, 1997.

Gower Street United Church: Once called "The Cathedral of Newfoundland Methodism," this Romanesque red brick building stands just across from the Anglican Cathedral, at the top of Church Hill. The building was opened in 1896, after the original church was destroyed in the fire of 1892. Its interior woodwork is made of pitch pine with a hammer-beamed roof, iron grillwork and over fifty stained glass windows including a large rose window.

St. John's : A BRIEF HISTORY

"The Kirk" St. Andrew's Presbyterian Church
RUSTED COLLECTION

Gower Street United Church
RUSTED COLLECTION

Cochrane Street United Church: Located at the top of Cochrane Street, Cochrane Street United Church is built in Romanesque Revival style. It has a unique appearance compared to the other churches in St. John's, with a 70 ft (21.5 m) high Mediterranean-style bell tower and 55 ft (17 m) high Byzantine dome supported by four Corinthian pillars. It was designated a Registered Historic Structure in 2004. The original Gothic church was destroyed by fire in 1914.

St. Patrick's Roman Catholic Church: Constructed of granite in early Gothic Revival style with massive circular pillars and pointed arches and completed in 1881, St. Patrick's is situated on Patrick Street in the west end of St. John's. The original 62 ft (19 m) steeple was removed in the spring of 1997 as it had become dangerous; it was replaced by an exact 11,500 lb (5,227 kg) replica from Utah in the fall of that year. It was given the Southcott Award in 1988. It was designated a National Historic Site in 1990, and the Heritage Foundation of Newfoundland and Labrador declared it a Registered Heritage Structure in 1997.

George Street United Church is the oldest surviving Methodist church in St. John's. George Street United Church, completed in 1873, is built in the Gothic Revival style in Newfoundland stone, faced with cement, and its roof is from slate quarried on the Southside Hills. It was designated a Heritage Structure in April 2000.

Wesley United Church: Built in 1908 in the Queen Anne and Romanesque styles, Wesley United Church is located on the corner of Patrick Street and Hamilton Avenue. It is home, in an adjacent building, to radio station VOWR (Voice Of Wesley Radio) 800AM, Newfoundland's oldest operating radio station, founded in 1928 and run by volunteers. The church was designated a Municipal Heritage structure.

The **Masonic Temple** was built on Cathedral Street in 1894 of Accrington brick upon a stone foundation. The three-storey building is a fine example of Victorian lodge construction. It contains classical motifs, pilasters and multiple pediments. The last Masonic meeting was held in 2007; the building was sold and has no further Masonic connections. It was designated a Heritage Structure in April 1995 and is listed in the Canadian Register of Historic Places.

St. Thomas' Anglican Church: The oldest standing church in St. John's, St. Thomas', opened in 1836 and was the official church of the Newfoundland Garrison until they withdrew in 1871. The church was moved six inches from its foundations in the Great Gale of 1846. Wings were then added on the north and south sides to secure the building. Many houses near the "Old Garrison Church" were constructed in Second Empire style and most of that area on Military Road survived the fire of 1892. The church was designated a National Historic Site in 1968, a Registered Heritage Structure in 1986 and given the Southcott Award in 1987.

St. Patrick's Roman Catholic Church
RUSTED COLLECTION

George Street United Church
RUSTED COLLECTION

The Masonic Temple
RUSTED COLLECTION

St. Thomas' Anglican Church
CITY OF ST. JOHN'S ARCHIVES

The Commissariat House was constructed in 1818-1819 to serve as the offices and residence of the Assistant Commissary General, and is located on King's Bridge Road near St. Thomas', the Old Garrison Church. It served as headquarters for the supply of provisions and services to the British military in St. John's. The Georgian style building has been restored and furnished in the 1830 period, and is open to the public in the summer with interpretive guides dressed in period costume. It has been designated a Provincial Historic Site.

Government House on Military Road was built by Governor Sir Thomas Cochrane as a residence for the governors of Newfoundland. Constructed of local red sandstone trimmed with English Portland stone, it was begun in 1827 and took five years to complete, costing three times the original estimate.

Commissariat House
RUSTED COLLECTION

The two-storey building consists of a centre block flanked by slightly lower wings on the east and west. The ceilings in its reception room and ballrooms were beautifully painted by a Polish prisoner, Alexander Pindikowski, who also painted frescoes on ceilings in the Colonial Building and Presentation Convent. His sentence was shortened by one month for his good work. Spacious grounds surround this somber residence, one of the few buildings in North America surrounded by a twelve-foot deep dry moat. It is a designated National Heritage Structure.

The building is still used as the private residence of the Lieutenant Governor of Newfoundland and Labrador. You can enter the grounds daily until dusk and sign the visitors' book in the front porch until 6 p.m., unless there are official functions scheduled.

Government House, Front Entrance
RUSTED COLLECTION

Colonial Building: Built of white limestone from Ireland in the Classical Revival (Neo-Classical) style with massive Ionic columns, the imposing Colonial Building was completed in 1850. The ceiling was painted by the Polish prisoner Alexander Pindikowski in 1880. The building housed the Legislature of Newfoundland and Labrador, and government offices from 1850-1960. The Provincial Archives, once located here, have been moved to The Rooms.

Colonial Building
RUSTED COLLECTION

The building was the site of the National Convention that led to Confederation with Canada. It is now a Provincial Historic Site and being restored to its former appearance.

The Court House was built to replace an earlier Court House on Market House Hill, the site of the produce market, post office and public gallows. The cornerstone was laid in 1901 by the Duke and Duchess of Cornwall. Completed in 1904, the Court House was constructed of red granite from the Southside Hills in Neo-Romanesque style. This imposing building, located on Water and Duckworth Streets, was once used as offices for the Colonial Secretary, the Cabinet and Prime Ministers of Newfoundland. The Court House is now used for judicial purposes, and because of its style and age was named a National Historic Site in 1980.

The Court House
PHOTOGRAPHER GARLAND STUDIO, CITY OF ST. JOHN'S ARCHIVES

The Murray Premises on Harbour Drive were built in the 1840s, escaped the fire of 1892, and are now a National Historic Site. Previously one of the oldest warehouses on the harbour front, these lovely renovated white stone buildings house specialty shops, offices and St. John's first boutique hotel with executive suites on the second floor and hotel rooms on the third and fourth floors.

The Murray Premises
RUSTED COLLECTION

Bank of British North America is an Italianate Classical Neo-Renaissance style building on Duckworth Street, built in 1849, after the 1846 fire, for St. John's first commercial bank. The original hipped roof was replaced by a mansard roof in 1885. The building was designated a National Heritage Structure in 1991, and awarded the Southcott Award for heritage restoration in 1994.

chapter four

THE PORT OF ST. JOHN'S

St. John's harbour is formed of a bay one and one-half miles (2.5 km) long and up to half a mile (1 km) wide, with a narrow shallow entrance leading to the Atlantic Ocean. The 500-600 ft (150-200 m) high cliffs protect the harbour from the Atlantic gales. The narrow entrance prevents large waves from penetrating the harbour and it is only during easterly storms that part of the harbour is somewhat affected. The waves usually break between Chain Rock and Pancake Rock, where the entrance is narrowest. The city is located on the north shore of the bay. The harbour has a tidal range of 2 to 4 feet (0.6-1.2 m), with a depth of 26 to 30 feet (8-9 m) at its 27 berths. There are over three miles (5 km) of berths around the harbour, with four berths for refueling.

The entrance to St. John's harbour as described in the 1786 logbook of HM *Pegasus*:

> "The entrance to St. John's Harbour forms a long and extremely narrow strait, but not very difficult of access. There are about twelve fathoms of water in the middle of the channel with … good anchorage ground. The most lofty perpendicular precipices arise to an amazing height, upon the north side; and the southern shore only appears less striking in its attitude, from its comparison with the opposite rocks."

ST. JOHN'S : A BRIEF HISTORY

Chain Rock, Battery, house with fish flakes
MARITIME HISTORY ARCHIVE

Throughout Newfoundland's history, the port had a role as service station of the North Atlantic. Fishing ships and fleets took on water, fuel, food and provisions. Fishing ships used the port for recreation for their crews. Repairs were done in port at the dry dock at the west end of the harbour. The harbour was a natural protection from the North Atlantic gales.

Finger piers and schooners in St. John's harbour
MARITIME HISTORY ARCHIVE

Before the days of the auxiliary engine, dories rowed by oarsmen towed schooners into St. John's harbour. Schooners anchored or tied up to the many wharves, with their sails drying in the sun, would be a typical scene in the harbour. It was said that one could almost walk across the harbour on the decks of schooners anchored there. Cargo was loaded and unloaded by stevedores. In the winter the harbour would sometimes freeze over and ships froze into the ice. The port was one of great importance to the Allies in World War I and II, supplying convoys on their transatlantic crossings. The gun placements at Fort Amherst and the attachments for the submarine nets across the mouth of the harbour are lasting testimonials to this part of our history.

Dories towing a schooner in St. John's harbour
CITY OF ST. JOHN'S ARCHIVES

Harbour Pilots: When a ship nears port it radios its port agent informing the time of arrival. The agent then contacts the harbour master who assigns a berth, informs the Coast Guard traffic manager, and a pilot boat is dispatched by the Atlantic Pilotage Authority. The pilot tug guides the ship to its berth. The pilot boat must be used by all foreign and most large local ships.

Modern ships use AIS (Automated Identification Systems). This system reports on which ships are in the harbour and their locations.

Harbour Reconstruction in the 1950s: In 1956, the federal Department of Public Works began a study to modernize the harbour. The port of St. John's had been prevented from efficient and economic operation for many reasons. For years progress of industry and business on the Avalon Peninsula had been adversely affected by the absence of overall planning and co-ordination of harbour developments, crowding and inadequacy of existing wharf facilities and lack of mechanical equipment. The harbour of St. John's became unable to compete with Halifax and Montreal in freight handling in the new age of mass production and bigger ships. The roads around the old harbour had been built for horses and not large trucks.

Access to the south side and a new general cargo pier in the west end with direct access to rail service was begun. Homes were removed from the south side, and a quarry started, from which one million tons of fill was used for the new work in 1965. The harbour was dredged; marginal wharves replaced old finger piers; a small boat basin was developed; new wharves were built for the Department of Transport, Canadian Coast Guard Regional Supply Base; and a four-lane service road was built on the north side. Twenty million dollars was spent to ensure the controlled flow of traffic necessary for a modern harbour. The harbour sewage system was also modernized, and new pipes laid to the fuel storage tanks on the Southside Hills.

The St. John's Port Authority is a federal agency responsible for the development and regulation of the harbour.

Modern St. John's Harbour: St. John's is now a modern year-round port catering to ships from around the world. The busy working waterfront accommodates fishing boats, longliners, trawlers, cargo ships, petroleum tankers, supply tugs, freighters, cruise ships and tour boats. The port brings vast amounts of business to St. John's each year. The 200-mile limit for the fishery has placed fishery patrol boats in the port. Containerized cargo, from the modernized terminal at the west end of the harbour, is the principal means of transport, with weekly shipping runs from St. John's to Halifax and Montreal.

The offshore oil and gas industry has had the most impact and is the fastest growing sector in the harbour. Most oil exploration, development and production, shipping and rigs are serviced from St John's. Food, water, materials, pipe and fuel are sent offshore from Harvey's Pier 14, 15 and 16.

Several high-rise office buildings and a hotel have been built on Water and Duckworth Streets and blend into the traditional landscape, making the city a mix of the old and new.

St. John's Dockyard (Newdock): St John's was always a centre of repair for seagoing vessels. Two million dollars was spent to modernize the dry dock in the 1920s. During World War II the dockyard worked around the clock to repair damaged ships. The dry dock can handle ships up to 170 m (558 ft) long for repair. A new syncrolift has been installed on the area next to the dry dock, lifting much larger ships out of the water for repair on the ground level. The 18-acre dockyard is equipped for heavy industrial and mechanical activities and offers a full range of support for all fabrication, maintenance and service requirements within the offshore and ship repair industries. One can view the working dockyard on the drive to Fort Amherst on the south side of the harbour.

AREAS OF INTEREST AROUND THE HARBOUR AND ST. JOHN'S

Cabot Tower: Located high upon Signal Hill, Cabot Tower was constructed in 1897 to observe the 400th anniversary of the discovery of Newfoundland by John Cabot and also to celebrate the 60th year of the reign of Queen Victoria. A little known fact is that another Cabot Tower was constructed at about the same time in Bristol, England. The observation deck on the roof of the Tower is an excellent viewing place and was used to fly the signalling flags to indicate the approach of ships to St. John's harbour. For many years a noon–day gun was fired from Cabot Tower to announce the time at midday. A very good Marconi exhibit and amateur radio station, VO1AA, are found in Cabot Tower. The Southcott Award for restoration was given to Cabot Tower in 1992.

Cabot Tower
RUSTED COLLECTION

Signal Hill: The 500 ft (155 m) high hill overlooking the Narrows was used for almost 300 years as a signalling station to announce the arrival of ships, both friendly and hostile, to the harbour. The earliest record is of a British garrison signalling post in 1704. Signals were sent from blockhouses until 1900, when Cabot Tower took over. Merchant firms had their own house flags to mark property and ships. The approach of commercial shipping became the most important part of the signalling system, with the flags of individual merchants being flown from a mast on Cabot Tower until 1958 to indicate the arrival of one of their ships. Signals gave crews time to get dock facilities ready and call crews of longshoremen to unload the incoming ships.

Signal Hill was made a National Historic Site on May 22, 1958, because of its early fortifications and Seven Years War battle site. At this time the access road was paved and a renovation program initiated which included the restoration of fortifications on the hill. Signal Hill offers breathtaking views of the city, harbour, Cape Spear and the Atlantic Ocean from its lookout and walkways. A drive up the hill at night to see the city with its twinkling lights is magnificent and a must for any visitor.

The North Head hiking trail, for the adventurous, leads from Cabot Tower down the front of the hill to Ross' Valley and around to the small village of the Battery. It also leads in the opposite direction past Ladies Lookout — the highest point — to Quidi Vidi Battery.

Guglielmo Marconi received the first transatlantic wireless signal, the letter "S" in Morse code, from England on December 12, 1901, on the top of Signal Hill in a vacant wing of a military barracks used as a hospital.

Quarantine Hospitals were located in converted barracks on Signal Hill, on the site of the existing parking lot, and used from 1842 until 1892 when the barracks were destroyed by fire. The hospitals then moved to other quarters and until 1920 were known as the Diphtheria and Fever Hospital and the Signal Hill Hospital.

Cabot Tower and Quarantine Hospital
COURTESY DR. N. RUSTED

Marine Hospital was built in Ross' Valley, the area below Signal Hill, in 1892 for smallpox victims and also for cholera. Patients from incoming vessels were to be sent to the hospital from the area near Chain Rock and therefore would not enter the city. The hospital was established by Judge Prowse and afterwards called Prowse's Folly as it was too isolated for many patients to reach. All of the hospitals were eventually destroyed by fire.

Jails: The abandoned military buildings were also used as the St. John's temporary jail or gaol from 1846 to 1879. The Great Fire had destroyed the jail in the Court House, and Signal Hill was used as the main detention centre for 13 years before a new penitentiary was built.

The **Signal Hill Interpretation Centre** preserves and interprets the history of military fortifications, signalling stations and medical facilities that served and protected St. John's. Audio visual presentations give the military history of St. John's.

GEO Centre and GEO Park: A museum and science centre, the Johnson GEO Centre "Earth's Geological Showcase" focuses on the geology of Newfoundland and Labrador and tells the story of the Earth using examples from the province. The centre is built on a 13-hectare property, into the rocks of Signal Hill. Visitors go underground from the upper entrance to see natural exposed rock walls as well as exhibits on geoscience and resource development. GEO also offers interpretative and educational programs to schools and universities as well as public tours. There are plans to expand the Kid Zone and for the completion of a new permanent exhibit on space. GEO also hosts many travelling exhibits throughout the year.

Also showcased are the *Titanic* story — a complete account of the tragedy just 350 miles (564 km) off Newfoundland — and the ExxonMobil Oil and Gas Gallery — a visual introduction to oil and gas exploration, drilling and production processes particularly relevant for Hibernia and the Grand Banks. The gallery features interactive stations and large-scale models of the Hibernia oil platform and floating production, storage and offloading vessels.

The GEO Centre has a new 3D theatre offering natural history and other films in its 76-seat theatre.

The GEO Park was opened in 2007 and provides eight interconnected walkways around the GEO Centre through spectacular natural rocks and plants with many breathtaking views. It features geological and botanical storyboard panels and natural stoneworks, all in an unmatched setting on historic Signal Hill.

George's Pond, on the higher level of Signal Hill, is spring fed and connected to the town's water supply as a backup. It was once the town's only water supply.

Gibbet Hill: Gibbeting was a relatively common practice in the 17th, 18th and early 19th centuries. The gibbet was used to display a body, which after execution was usually dipped in boiling tar, wrapped in chains, and hung until it decomposed and fell apart. The first gibbet in St. John's was near the bottom of Prescott Street and moved in 1759 to Gibbet Hill, a prominent point on Signal Hill. This area was formerly named Crow's Nest on old maps of St. John's. The bodies were hung in this prominent place as an example of what could happen to lawbreakers. Folklore has it that the bodies were removed from the gibbets, weighed down and dumped into Deadman's Pond. The gibbet was torn down in 1796 to make way for Wallace's Battery.

The Battery: In the early days this fishing village within the city contained fish flakes and sheds used in the fishery, as well as homes of many fishermen. Its name originated from the guns situated there and on other points of the hills overlooking the Narrows, protecting the port of St. John's from attack by pirates and warships. This area has become a popular place to live because of its superb harbour view, village atmosphere and brightly coloured houses.

Making fish on flakes at the Battery, circa 1900
MARY SOUTHCOTT PHOTOGRAPH, COURTESY DR. N. RUSTED

Maggoty Cove: The area east of the Port of St. John's Administration Building on Water Street, at the bottom of Temperance Street, was known as Maggoty Cove. It contained large numbers of fish flakes where fish was "made" (cured). With an outbreak of poor weather, fish, especially capelin, produced maggots. Those that fell through the boughs or long sticks from the flakes to the path or road below gave the name to this historic part of town. When the flakes were taken down the name of the area was changed to Hoyles Town, after a prominent premier and chief justice of the time, Sir Hugh Hoyles.

Monkey's Puzzle: The winding path under the long sticks supporting the fish flakes at Maggoty Cove, which led from the foot of Signal Hill, was called Monkey's Puzzle. Some say that people lived in this area under the flakes.

Quidi Vidi Lake and the **Royal St. John's Regatta:** The Regatta at Quidi Vidi Lake, started in 1826, is the oldest continuous annual sporting event in North America. It is held on the first Wednesday in August, weather permitting. It brings a full day of team races in racing shells on the "pond," amid much friendly rivalry. The day is a municipal holiday and throngs of people line the lake to view the races and enjoy the festivities. Quidi Vidi Battery and Quidi Vidi Village are only a short distance away.

Harbourside Park and **Gilbert Memorial:** Harbourside Park is a commemorative site on King's Beach. Sir Humphrey Gilbert landed there in 1583 and claimed possession of Newfoundland as Britain's first colony. The park was developed by the Johnson Family Foundation and expanded by its present owner, the St. John's Port Authority. It is a fascinating place to visit and view the harbour activities. Statues entitled *Our Dogs* look out over the harbour. Lunchtime concerts are held here in the summertime.

Maggoty Cove before fire of 1892
CITY OF ST. JOHN'S ARCHIVES

Maggoty Cove after fire of 1892
CITY OF ST. JOHN'S ARCHIVES

Unveiling of the War Memorial in St. John's by Field Marshall Haig,
July 1, 1924
RUSTED COLLECTION

The Provincial War Memorial: The War Memorial is situated adjacent to Harbourside Park. The memorial was unveiled by Field Marshall Haig on July 1, 1924, on the eighth anniversary of the Battle of the Somme, to commemorate the Newfoundlanders who died in the First World War. Engravings were later added to remember those who served and died in World War II and more current conflicts. The War Memorial area was known as Haymarket for activities that took place there. Today, offices, restaurants and a bar are located nearby in a renovated building named Haymarket Square. The Old Customs House was located on the site of the War Memorial. Its foundations were uncovered during the Harbour Interceptor Project for the new sewage treatment plant on the south side.

Harvey's Pier 14, 15 & 16 is a service centre for offshore oil and gas exploration, development and production, shipping and rigs. Food, water, materials, pipe and fuel are sent offshore.

Crow's Nest: Located on Water Street next to the War Memorial, the Crow's Nest is a private Seagoing Officers Club dating from 1941-1942 when it was open to officers of the Allied fighting ships and the merchant navy. It is reached by a small alley on the steps to Duckworth Street northeast of the War Memorial. The name "Crow's Nest" is said to originate from the 59-step steep climb to the club. The walls are covered with military artifacts and memorabilia. It is famous for having a periscope rising from its roof that came from a German submarine that surrendered at Bay Bulls at the end of WWII. The club is open to past and present naval officers and their guests. It was recognized as a Registered Heritage Structure in April 1990.

LSPU Hall: Built in 1923, the large timber-framed Long-shoremen's Protective Union meeting hall on Victoria Street off Duckworth Street is now an active Resource Centre for the Arts (RCA). The hall underwent extensive restoration and opened again in 2010 with a new and improved interior space complete with new theatre seats and air conditioning in its intimate 200-seat theatre. The RCA is a nonprofit organization committed to the advancement of the performing arts in Newfoundland and Labrador with its own house RCA Theatre Company. The centre's mandate is to produce and promote emerging local artists, and hosts music, theatre and dance ranging from the experimental to the traditional. The hall was given the Southcott Award in 1984 and recognized as a Registered Heritage Structure in October 1988.

The Rooms: The Provincial Museum, Archives and Art Gallery are located in this visually striking building that dominates the St. John's skyline. Its distinctive design combines the "fishing rooms" of the past with 21st century technology.

The Rooms' distinctive, brightly coloured gabled roofs evoke images of the past while the modern glass atrium offers panoramic views of St. John's, allowing for a captivating view of the city and making the cityscape a part of the artwork.

The Rooms' 185,000 square feet encompasses five main exhibition galleries, a 121-seat multimedia theatre, nine climate-controlled vaults, as well as four permanent classrooms that support various educational programs.

The Rooms was built on the site of Fort Townshend, the 18th century star-shaped citadel, one of the largest British fortifications in North America. Careful research and documentation before construction ensured that future study of the site is possible. Future plans for The Rooms call for the development of an exterior site that will include the demarcation of Fort Townshend.

The Rooms Provincial Museum: The Rooms Provincial Museum Division's large collection is arranged in four broad categories: archaeology/ethnology, social history, natural history and military history. There are more than one million archaeological items, an impressive array of native artifacts, the world's largest Beothuk collection, as well as more than one million natural history specimens, some of which include internationally significant "voucher" specimens that serve as benchmarks to scientific classification.

Provincial Archives:
With a mandate to collect and preserve a record of life in Newfoundland and Labrador, The Rooms Provincial Archives Division holds documents

The Rooms
IMAGE PROVIDED COURTESY OF
THE ROOMS

dating from 1630; its vaults contain everything from government records to ships' logs, and diaries to church meeting reports. The Archives are the province's only record of births, baptisms, marriages, and deaths.

Its collection includes over 400,000 photographs, some 50,000 maps, records and diaries of colonial secretaries, governors and prime ministers, post-confederation government records, as well as merchant and business records of the colony and country. Its textual records, if stacked side by side, would stretch nearly seven kilometres (4.35 miles).

The Archives provides online searching capability for distance clients, as well as a 4,600 square-foot research room that makes a comfortable physical environment for on-site client researchers, including legal professionals, writers, artists, genealogists, filmmakers, academics, local historians and the general public.

Provincial Art Gallery: The Rooms Provincial Art Gallery Division manages a collection of over 8,000 works, ranging from historical, contemporary and international art, to crafts and folk art. While concentrating on Newfoundland and Labrador artists, the collection includes many other Canadian works, including a Jean-Paul Riopelle painting valued at $1.8 million.

Comprising 10,000 square feet of gallery space for permanent collections and travelling exhibitions, the gallery provides visitors with a diverse program of local, national and international art.

> As an emblem of provincial passion and pride, and through the expertise of The Rooms Provincial Archives, Art Gallery and Museum Divisions, The Rooms has become "one of the most compelling and amazing cultural museums of its size in the world."
>
> – Emily Wolman, *Lonely Planet Publications*

City Hall, built into a slope on the north side of New Gower Street, was officially opened in 1970. A new annex — the John J. Murphy Building, connected via a skywalk — was built on the south side of the street. The buildings house the council

St. John's

chambers, mayor's office, as well as municipal and administrative offices. Other offices throughout the city include a tourist information centre located at 348 Water Street.

St. John's was incorporated as a city in 1921 with the passage of the City of St. John's Act. The city is governed by an elected mayor, elected deputy mayor and nine elected councillors serving four-year terms.

Terry Fox began his Marathon of Hope cross-Canada run in April 1980 at Mile '0' of the Trans-Canada Highway in front of City Hall. A monument to Terry Fox is now located near the St. John's Port Authority Building at 1 Water Street.

A *Chinese Head Tax* monument is located in the annex courtyard. This monument commemorates the 334 Chinese male immigrants who paid a $300 head tax to the Dominion of Newfoundland between 1906 and 1949. Storyboards give a brief history of Chinese immigrants to Newfoundland as well as photographs from local archives.

Mile One Centre: Located on New Gower Street next to City Hall, the Mile One Centre is a sports and entertainment centre built in 2001 to replace Memorial Stadium. It seats 6,250 for hockey games and has a full capacity of 8,000. The venue showcases the arts, live entertainment, community events, trade shows and sporting events. Adjacent are the **St. John's Convention Centre** and Delta Hotel, both accessible by skywalk.

A statue, *Making Fish,* is located in front of the Convention Centre.

Southside Hills: The hills are of a higher elevation than Signal Hill, both protecting the harbour from the fury of the Atlantic Ocean and providing natural fortification against enemy attack. Fishing rooms, stages, wharves and warehouses were located on this side of the harbour until the 20th century when the south side began to emerge as an industrial area of St. John's with seal oil factories and docks to load and unload coal, fish and salt. There were almost 1,300 residents in 1911. The population continued to increase until the 1940s. The Canadian Army built two barracks during World War II. Oil tanks were built into the hills and houses torn down to improve docking. By the end of the war the population had begun to decline, and when the harbour was reconstructed between 1959 and 1964, many houses were torn down and the hill dynamited to widen the road and provide fill. Residents still live in the area closest to the Narrows.

During the south side reconstruction, **St. Mary's Church** was torn down and a piece of Newfoundland history was lost. The graveyard had been dismantled in 1903 for railway construction. A monument near the site, taken down during the construction of the new wastewater treatment plant and awaiting a new location, read:

> "This monument marks the site of the Parish Church of St. Mary the Virgin during the period 1859-1963. Fishermen and sailors from many ports found a spiritual haven within its hallowed walls. Near this spot is the burying place of Nancy Shanawdithit, very probably the last of the Beothuks, who died on June 6, 1829."

A small monument to **Shanawdithit** was placed in Bannerman Park in 2008.

The Beothuk were the native inhabitants of Newfoundland when the Europeans arrived. Hunters and fisher-gatherers, they came to the coast in the spring to catch fish, seals, salmon and gather eggs. They wintered in the interior, hunting herds of caribou. The long-held theory is that, with European settlement, they found it difficult to come to the coastline to use coastal resources and became extinct from a combination of starvation, European diseases, and direct killings by settlers. Shanawdithit was found, near starvation, in 1823 by trappers from the Exploits Bay area. She was brought to St. John's by the Beothuk Institution in 1828 and lived in St. John's for the last six months of her life, staying with William E. Cormack and later, at the house of James Simms. She died from tuberculosis in 1829.

The **Coast Guard Regional Agency** is located on this side of the harbour, as well as a refueling centre for boats, a **Marine Institute training centre** and dock, a **power substation** and the new **sewage treatment plant**. Oil storage tanks are situated high upon the hill, away from the city. Old metal doors on the base of the hill lead to caves where gunpowder was stored and later liquor aged for the Newfoundland Liquor Corporation.

Prosser's Rock Small Boat Basin: The federal government moved small fishing boats from the west end of the harbour to their new location in the Narrows at a cost of seven million dollars. The old basin at Riverhead frequently silted up and was becoming crowded with fishermen. Fort Amherst, the old lighthouse and WW I fortifications are located a short distance from here.

Riverhead Wastewater Treatment Facility on the south side is now fully operational. The City of St. John's, the City of Mount Pearl and the Town of Paradise have a combined population of over 130,000 people. Municipal wastewater from these municipalities was previously discharged, untreated, into St. John's harbour; 700,000 cubic metres of material was removed from the site on Southside Road to facilitate construction of the new plant. A new 2 km (1.2 mile) Harbour Interceptor Sewer was constructed to bypass the St. John's harbour. The total project cost exceeded $137 million.

Riverhead Hospital: The first general hospital was built in St. John's in 1813 at Riverhead. It was used until 1888 when it became uninhabitable and was burnt. The hospital then moved to the old **Military Hospital** on Forest and Quidi Vidi Roads. The name later changed to the **General Hospital**.

The General Hospital moved to the new **Health Sciences Complex** on Prince Philip Drive in 1978. The old hospital on Forest Road was renamed the **Dr. L.A. Miller Centre** for convalescence and rehabilitation and the **Caribou Pavilion** wing for Veterans. The **Lillian Stevenson Nursing Archives and Museum** is located at the Dr. L.A. Miller Centre. It is a hospital medical nursing archives/museum with a collection of hospital artifacts from earlier days of medical and nursing practices in Newfoundland.

Cape Spear: The most easterly point in North America, Cape Spear is a short distance by car from St. John's, and a spectacular scene to be viewed during a boat tour outside the harbour. Drive southwest along Water Street, turn left at Leslie Street and look for the sign to Cape Spear.

There are two lighthouses at Cape Spear; the original is the oldest existing lighthouse in Newfoundland. It was built in 1835 and in service until 1955, manned by the Cantwell family. The old lighthouse is now a museum and displays the 19th century dwelling of the lightkeeper and his family. The original light had seven great lenses and reflectors, lit by whale oil lamps. The new lighthouse was built in 1955.

Cape Spear was of strategic importance during World War II, with coastal battery fortifications built to defend the entrance of St. John's harbour against U-boats. The two large gun emplacements can still be seen there. The panoramic view is magnificent at Cape Spear National Historic Park. You can look out at the endless Atlantic, see Signal Hill and the entrance to St. John's harbour, watch the seabirds, and look for whales and icebergs in season. You are closer, at this point, to Europe than to the centre of Canada.

You can access the East Coast Trail from the parking lot at Cape Spear.

Sprigg's Point is a black-legged kittiwake bird sanctuary. The looming rocky shoreline is the nesting grounds of these small swallow-winged seagulls that lay their eggs on narrow ledges and in crevices. Boat tours from the St. John's harbour cruise by the spectacular rock formations to observe and listen to these birds in their natural habitat.

The Railway: St. John's original railway station was on the site of Fort William near the present Sheraton Hotel Newfoundland.

The first rail line ran along what is now Empire Avenue. There was also a spur line at Hoyles Town in the east end at the present site of the "Army dock" near the St. John's Port Authority building. The 1898 contract with the Reid Newfoundland Company centralized all operations in the west end of St. John's harbour. Railway and machine sheds were moved from Whitbourne to St. John's and a new rail line was built in the west end to replace the old track on Empire Avenue. A new railway station, constructed of granite, was built in 1910 at the west end of Water Street.

The area was adjacent to **Riverhead**, a large pond divided by a bridge and part of St. John's harbour. A large part of the area was later filled in to extend the rail lines and build sheds. The Reid Newfoundland Company operated the railway until 1923 when the government took over operation of the rail line and coastal shipping.

The railway was known to locals as the "Newfie Bullet," because of its lack of speed. It was said people could get off at the front of the train, pick some berries and get back on again at the caboose! The 537 mile (1,100 km) trip across the island from St. John's to Port aux Basques took 27 hours — an average speed of 20 miles (33 km) an hour.

Completed in 1898, the rail lines were built with light narrow gauge rails, allowing the trains to make tight turns in the steep, rocky areas. These rails did not permit the faster speeds or larger loads of the wider gauge railroads on the mainland. The railway, in accordance with the Terms of Union with Confederation with Canada was to be kept up, but sadly came to an end in July 1969 as it had become uneconomical to operate. The final trip was on September 20, 1988, and work began on dismantling the old narrow gauge rail lines. The rail beds are now mainly used for all-terrain vehicles, snowmobiles and other recreational purposes.

After the shutdown of the railway, the old Victorian station was, for several years, the home of the CN bus terminal. But, with the sale of that operation to private enterprise, the Newfoundland Railway Station was later purchased from the city in 2002 by the Johnson Family Foundation and restored to its original appearance. The Railway Coastal Museum was opened there in June 2003. The Railway Coastal Museum was given the Southcott Award for restoration in 2004.

The statue *Woman of Industry* stands at the front of the building.

The **Railway Coastal Museum** tells the story of the Newfoundland Railway and Coastal Services and how they were crucial for travel, mail, freight and healthcare for the thousands of Newfoundlanders who lived in the isolated and remote outports and settlements along the vast coastlines of Newfoundland and Labrador. The sea was the main highway until the railway opened up the interior to development, forestry and mining.

The station showcases over 100 exhibits and displays highlighting the 100-year history of the railway and coastal boats in

An early photograph of the Railway Station on Water Street West
COURTESY RAILWAY COASTAL MUSEUM

Newfoundland. The museum occupies the ground floor and railway platform and also houses the City Archives and Records on its upper two floors, as well as social rooms for Canadian National pensioners provided by the city.

A locomotive and railway cars reside outside the building in a railway park. Mile "Zero" of the Trans-Canada T'Rail (the old rail bed) is located nearby — a good photo opportunity.

Tommy Ricketts Monument: A monument to Tommy Ricketts and his family stands on the corner of Water and Job Streets across from the Railway Coastal Museum. Tommy was 15 when he enlisted in World War I. He was one of two Newfoundlanders to win the Victoria Cross in the war, and was also awarded the French Croix de Guerre. He returned from the war, trained as a pharmacist and opened a drugstore in this location. (The other Newfoundlander awarded the Victoria Cross was John Croak — born in Newfoundland but moved to Nova Scotia when he was two.)

Apothecary Hall: The James O'Mara Pharmacy Museum is located on Water Street West. It is a replica of a working apothecary in the 1889 era. The building was designated a Registered Heritage Structure and received the Southcott Award for restoration in 1988. The Newfoundland Pharmaceutical Association received a certificate of commendation in 1989 by the American Association of State and Local History for preservation of the history of pharmacy in Newfoundland.

Memorial University Complex: The old Memorial University College was located on the site of the Fort Townshend Parade Grounds on Parade Street. It opened in 1925 with a student population of 55. The college was established as a memorial to Newfoundland's war dead and veterans of the First World War and later encompassed those of the Second World War. The college was admitted to university status in 1949. The university moved to its new campus on Elizabeth Avenue and Prince Philip Drive in 1961.

Memorial has grown rapidly and is one of the city's major employers. The St. John's campus covers approximately 220 acres. The university has six Faculties: Arts, Science, Education, Medicine, Engineering and Business; and seven Schools: Graduate Studies, Nursing, Human Kinetics and Recreation, Social Work, Continuing Studies, Music, and Pharmacy. It also offers degree programs in Fine Arts. The university has an excellent reputation in engineering, business, geology, and medicine and is one of the top comprehensive universities in Canada. There are now approximately 17,500 full and part-time students in Memorial's faculties and professional schools.

The university library is one of the best in Canada and holds in excess of three million volumes on its shelves. Researchers in St. John's and around the world avail of the library's branches: the main Queen Elizabeth II Library, the Health Sciences Library and the Marine Institute Library. The Queen Elizabeth II Library houses the Centre for Newfoundland Studies, which contains specialized collections, many old and rare, and the largest collection of published Newfoundlandiana anywhere. The Maritime History Archive, located in the Henrietta Harvey Building, holds records and information relating to maritime industries and culture. These records document shipping, sea-farers, fishermen, the fishing industry and shipwrecks. Records are also available for those studying family history and genealogy.

The Marine Institute is a post-secondary ocean and marine polytechnic, associated with Memorial University. It offers degrees, diplomas, certifications and industry training in marine and fisheries technology. The institute has a full mission bridge simulator, the world's largest flume tank, an aquaculture facility, fully equipped and licensed food processing facility, marine diesel labs and a planetarium.

Many special divisions have been established at MUN over the years to meet the expanding needs of the province.

The Ocean Sciences Centre: Scientists at the cold water research facility, located in Logy Bay, conduct research on the North Atlantic fishery, aquaculture, oceanography, ecology, behaviour and physiology. From June to August a summer visitors' program allows visitors to view the outdoor touch tank, seal compound, and learn about the marine environment and research.

The National Research Council's **Institute for Marine Dynamics** and the **Centre for Cold Ocean Resources Engineering** are also affiliated with Memorial.

Centre for Earth Resources Research (CERR), a unit of Memorial University's Earth Sciences Department, has a mandate "to collaborate with industry and government on matters related to earth resources." Many earth science facilities, including the Alexander Murray Building, were made possible by a $27 million contribution from the Canada-Newfoundland Offshore Development Fund (ODF) to "develop provincial infrastructure needed to take advantage of opportunities associated with the Hibernia oil play on the Grand Banks of Newfoundland." CERR uses the "department's research expertise and equipment to develop a more viable provincial private sector," acting as the interface between the department and private and public sectors. CERR also offers professional development and training which convey the latest university research developments into the private sector.

Grenfell Campus, Memorial University of Newfoundland, was established in Corner Brook in 1975. Programs are offered in the Arts, Fine Arts, including Theatre and Visual Arts, Science, Nursing and Education.

Memorial also established a small residential campus in **Harlow, England.** It provides accommodation for students and academic staff while they gain field experience in the United Kingdom and also acts as a base for teaching credit courses.

The **Health Sciences Centre** was opened in 1978 to house the General Hospital and a new Faculty of Medicine. It has since been expanded to house the School of Nursing, Janeway Children's Health and Rehabilitation Centre, the Dr. H. Bliss Murphy Cancer Centre and the Agnes Cowan Hostel.

MUN Botanical Garden is Memorial University's 44-hectare (109-acre) nature reserve, research facility, public garden and education centre. With colourful gardens, 3.5 km (2.2 miles) of nature trails and native plant collections, the botanical garden is located on 306 Mt. Scio Road.

Confederation Building: The Provincial House of Assembly was transferred from the Colonial Building to the new Confederation Building on Prince Philip Drive in 1960. The building houses government offices, and a new West Block annex was completed in 1986 using brick from Trinity Bay. Joseph Smallwood wanted to centralize the government, university, a theatre and hospital in the same area, built on land from Pippy Park. The new House of Assembly Chamber was completed in 1991; it outgrew its former location on the top floor. Newfoundland is the only province where government employees work in the same location as the House of Assembly.

The lobby contains many interesting articles and a mural by the late Harold Goodridge — an allegorical representation of Confederation depicting Newfoundland's past and future. Sixty-eight banners on the walls represent every Royal Canadian Legion in the province. A replica *Newfoundland Book of Remembrance* is displayed, identical to the one in the Memorial Chamber of the Parliament Buildings in Ottawa. The book lists the names of Newfoundlanders killed in military service in both World Wars: two pages of names are opened each day. On request one can view a small book listing all the names and can also find out the dates when each page will be open in the large book. The *Newfoundland Book of Remembrance* can now also be accessed online via Memorial University's website.

Free 20-minute tours of the House of Assembly leave the main lobby during weekdays when the House is not in session.

Arrangements can be made through the Sergeant-at-Arms located in the main lobby.

The grounds contain statues of John Cabot, Sir Wilfred Grenfell, Gaspar Corte Real, a monument to the *Ocean Ranger* — a disaster in which the oil rig went down in a storm on February 15, 1982, with a loss of eighty-four lives — a monument to mark the 10th anniversary of the Northern Cod Moratorium on July 2, 2002, a Peace Memorial honouring those Newfoundlanders and Labradorians who died on any battlefield, and the large polished granite Provincial Coat of Arms and lookout erected on the front grounds of the building — donated by the Johnson Family Foundation.

As with the statue of our Lady of Fatima at the Basilica, the statue of Corte Real was an indication of the long-standing friendship between Newfoundland and Portugal. In 1965 the bronze statue of the explorer, who visited Labrador in 1500-1502, was donated to the Government of Newfoundland and Labrador by the Portuguese government and placed in position in front of the Confederation Building overlooking the harbour. The inscription reads:

> "Gaspar Corte Real, Portuguese Navigator. He reached Terra Nova in the fifteenth century at the beginning of an era of great discoveries. From the Portuguese Fisheries Organization as an expression of gratitude on the behalf of the Portuguese Grand Banks fishermen for the friendly hospitality always extended to them by the people of Terra Nova — May 1965."

Arts & Culture Centre: The centre, located in Pippy Park on Prince Philip Drive, houses libraries, an art gallery, a 1,007-seat Main Theatre, and a 75-seat Basement Theatre. Opened in 1967, the centre was the province's major centennial project, built on the site of the former Church of England Boys' Orphanage. The centre offers a wide variety of programs including the best of local, national and international artists, and hosts approximately 100,000 patrons each year.

CITY PARKS

Bannerman Park: Located next to the Colonial Building in the heart of St John's, Bannerman Park was opened in 1891 by Governor of Newfoundland Sir Alexander Bannerman, who donated the land from part of the Government House grounds. The park contains a swimming pool, baseball diamond, playground, large trees and open grassy areas. It is the location of many festivals and events such as the Newfoundland & Labrador Folk Festival and is the finish for the famous "Tely 10" ten-mile road race held in July — one of the oldest road races in Canada.

Victoria Park: Located in the west end of Water Street, Victoria Park was established in the late 1800s. It is a Colonial style park with large tree-lined paths and colourful flower beds. A Lantern Festival takes place on the last Saturday of each July.

Bowring Park is located in the west end of the city on Waterford Bridge Road. The land was donated to St. John's by the Bowrings — one of the city's most prominent business families. The park was opened in 1914 to commemorate the centennial of Bowring Brothers Limited. The park is in a beautiful natural setting with walkways, streams, swans and ducks, flowers, a swimming pool and playground. It contains three interesting bronze statues, two of which are memorials to the World War I dead of the Royal Newfoundland Regiment. *The Fighting Newfoundlander* is a full

Peter Pan – "In Memory of Betty Munn, a Dear Little Girl Who Loved the Park"
RUSTED COLLECTION

life-sized statue of a soldier in full battle kit in the act of throwing a grenade. *The Caribou*, a life-sized statue of the emblem of the Regiment, is a replica of a statue at Beaumont Hamel in France. Replicas of the bronze plaques at Beaumont Hamel, memorializing Newfoundland's war dead who have no known graves, were erected in 2009. *Peter Pan* was given to the park by Sir Edgar Bowring in memory of his godchild who drowned at sea. The bronze statue is an exact replica, from the same mould, of the original in Kensington Gardens, London.

Pippy Park, the largest park in St. John's, covering about 3,400 acres (1,375 hectares), was established in 1968 to set aside land for the planned expansion of the Provincial Government and Memorial University. The park stretches across the northern portion of the city and includes many institutional facilities including the Confederation Building, Memorial University Campus, the College of the North Atlantic, the Health Sciences Hospital Complex and the Arts and Culture Centre.

Based on the vision of then Premier Joseph Smallwood and local philanthropist Chesley A. Pippy, the parkland has evolved into one of the most diverse urban parks in Canada with facilities such as a modern full service campground and trailer park, two golf courses, banquet and meeting clubhouse, numerous walking trails and playgrounds. The northern-most portion of the park borders on the city watershed and includes natural barrens and woodlands that can be enjoyed year round by hikers and cross-country skiers. One of the best tourist attractions in the park is the Suncor Fluvarium.

Pippy Park is almost completely surrounded by residential development; however, it provides numerous all-season recreational opportunities right on everyone's doorstep. In the winter the roads and trails of the campsite are used for cross-country skiing, you can skate on Long Pond and toboggan on the slopes leading down to it. St. John's is one of the few cities where these winter activities can be enjoyed so close to home.

Fluvarium: The Suncor Energy Fluvarium centre has a 25 m (82 ft) fluvarium — a series of underwater viewing windows built into the bed of Nagle's Hill Brook, where one can see a panoramic view of underwater stream life, brook and brown trout in their natural environment. This lovely octagonal wooden building, the only public fluvarium in North America, is located on the shore of Long Pond in Pippy Park, off Higgin's Line near the Confederation Building. The facility is a project of the Quidi Vidi/Rennie's River Development Foundation, funded by Suncor Energy, formerly Petro Canada, and is open year round.

HIKING TRAILS

Many first-class hiking trails have been developed in and around the St. John's area, making St. John's one of the most hiker friendly cities in North America.

Signal Hill North Head Trail, a hiking trail for the adventurous, leads from Cabot Tower almost 500 feet (152 m) down the front of the hill over stairs, boardwalks and a footpath to Ross' Valley and around to the small village of the Lower Battery. A path also leads in the opposite direction past Ladies Lookout — the highest point on Signal Hill — to Quidi Vidi Battery. See the sun rise over the Atlantic Ocean. There are spectacular views of the Atlantic Ocean, the Narrows, the harbour and the city from this trail.

Rennie's River Hiking Trail: This scenic trail extends from the Fluvarium at Pippy Park to Quidi Vidi Lake and picturesque Quidi Vidi village. Its pathways and boardwalks follow along the river and offer an enjoyable outing through the centre of the city. It is now part of the Grand Concourse.

East Coast Trail: A world class hiking trail, called by a visitor "one of the hiking world's greatest secrets," follows the winding Atlantic coastline from Fort Amherst in St. John's to Cappahayden on the southern shore. This 220 km (137 mile) section is equipped with signage, maps and supporting information. It consists of a series of 18 paths with distinctively marked northern and southern trailheads. There are entry points from all communities along the way. Some paths are easy walks and others are longer and more challenging. Purchase of East Coast Trail Maps is recommended to locate trailheads, learn about distances and understand the trail ratings.

A further 320 km (200 miles) of trails are under development and not yet supported with maps and signs. These sections include the northeastern tip of the Avalon Peninsula from St. John's to Topsail Beach and the southeastern tip from Cappahayden to Trepassey. A section from Pouch Cove to Flat Rock is now fully developed.

Experience 100 metre (328 ft) cliffs, forgotten villages, **the Spout** — a natural geyser that erupts 20 metres (66 ft) high. View whales, seabirds and icebergs in season, lighthouses, an archeological dig, tidal pools, boreal forests and quiet solitude. The trail links over 30 communities, some of which offer grocery stores, bed and breakfasts and adventure tour companies. Be prepared for changes in the weather!

Grand Concourse Trails: The Grand Concourse Authority partnership was formed with the resources of three levels of government, Memorial University and the Johnson Family Foundation to "beautify the capital region and showcase specific heritage and natural assets." A series of urban walkways and amenities connect most major attractions, historic sites, parks, the Fluvarium, ponds and river systems in St. John's and the neighbouring City of Mount Pearl and Town of Paradise.

Newfoundland T'Railway: The old rail bed, known as the Newfoundland T'Railway Provincial Park, extends for 883 km (548 miles), linking urban, rural and wilderness areas and forms the Newfoundland section of the Trans-Canada T'Rail stretching from the Atlantic Ocean to the Pacific Ocean and up to the Arctic. Once completed, the trail will extend for more than 22,000 km (13,680 miles) — the longest continuous trail in the world. The T'Rail Park is open to hikers, cyclists, horse-back riders, snowmobiles, ATV riders, and for cross-country skiing but not onroad motorised vehicles.

THE ARTS AND MUSIC SCENE

The City of St. John's was designated a **Cultural Capital of Canada** in 2006. The city has many fine artists, art galleries, musicians — both classical and traditional — writers, theatre and film. Funding to assist artists, musicians, and writers is available through associations such as the Newfoundland and Labrador Arts Council, Canada Council, the Government of Canada, the Government of Newfoundland and Labrador and St. John's City Council.

"Music has always been at the centre of a Newfoundlander's identity. More recently, St. John's has earned the reputation of Canada's hippest place for new music. Many Newfoundland bands are touring the world and they're winning awards. Most of them cut their teeth on tiny George Street in St. John's. There are more bars per square metre there than anywhere in North America."

– Kevin Newman,
"St. John's Music Scene,"
Global News Transcripts, Toronto:
Sept. 7, 2009

A Time by Morgan MacDonald, 2008 – arts sculpture to celebrate the contribution of the arts to the City of St. John's and also to commemorate St. John's being designated a Cultural Capital of Canada
RUSTED COLLECTION

The Eastern Edge Gallery, an artist-run gallery, and St. Michael's Printshop, an artist-run print studio that provides printmaking facilities for emerging and established artists, are located in downtown St. John's. Many local galleries showcase works of local artists, as well as Canadian and international art. Excellent professional photographers' galleries display local landscapes and seascapes.

Newfoundland and Labrador Books: The province is recognized for its vibrant literary tradition. St. John's has a higher per capita number of published writers than any other city in Canada. Books written by authors from Newfoundland and Labrador regularly appear on the short lists for international and national literary awards such as the Dublin Impac award, the Scotiabank Giller prize, the Canadian Authors' Association awards, the Governor General's awards and the Atlantic book awards. Each year the Winterset Award recognizes the best book published by a Newfoundland and Labrador author. The Writers' Alliance of Newfoundland and Labrador (WANL), in partnership with the Literary Arts Foundation of Newfoundland and Labrador, sponsors literary awards (fiction and children's literature in one year; poetry and non-fiction in the following year), and the two organizations also give the Fresh Fish Award to the best unpublished manuscript by a Newfoundland and Labrador writer. In partnership with the Historic Sites Association, WANL presents a Heritage and History Book Award for a work of fiction, non-fiction, poetry or young adult/children's literature each year. The Newfoundland and Labrador Arts Council encourages emerging writers by providing awards for unpublished short stories, plays, poems, and novels each year in both adult and junior divisions.

The **SPARKS Literary Festival,** sponsored by Memorial University of Newfoundland and featuring both established and emerging writers, is held in St. John's in January. The Winterset in Summer Literary Festival, The March Hare, and Writers at Woody Point are just a few of the literary festivals held in Newfoundland each year.

Theatre: The 1950s and 1960s produced a strong theatre tradition with the presence of the London Theatre Company and the upsurge of amateur theatrical companies. The Arts and Culture Centre and its Basement Theatre opened in St. John's in 1967, providing larger venues for productions.

A burst of theatre developed in the 1970s. The Newfoundland Travelling Theatre Company (NTTC) was formed in 1972, touring across the province and bringing classical theatre and plays by Newfoundland writers to communities and schools. Many people connected with NTTC went on to join or form other companies such as the Mummers Troupe, CODCO and the Rising Tide Theatre. Their success sowed the seeds of expansion into the vibrant theatre of today. Newfoundland gained a national reputation for its talent. The Mummers Troupe revived the *Christmas Mummers Play,* keeping old mummering traditions alive at Christmastime.

Recognizing the need for open access to an innovative and developmental arts centre, the St. John's theatre community opened the now legendary LSPU Hall in 1976. It quickly became a central force in the province's arts scene and in its early years was arguably the National Theatre of Newfoundland.

The Resource Centre for the Arts Theatre Company is currently the resident troupe of the LSPU Hall.

The Rising Tide Theatre, an off-shoot of the Mummers Troupe, presents a popular annual revue-style sketch of comedies at arts and culture centres across the province and each summer in Trinity an historical *Trinity Pageant* and *Summer in the Bight Theatre Festival* showcasing Newfoundland plays.

New companies have formed: Artistic Fraud, Rabbittown Theatre Company, Newfoundland ArtistX (based at the Rabbittown Theatre), C2C (based at the Basement Theatre), She Said Yes Theatre Company, Andy Jones Productions, Amyhouse, Wonderbolt Productions and many other talented independent groups.

Newfoundland and Labrador's actors and playwrights have won Gemini, Genie, ACTRA and Earl Grey Awards, as well as the

Simonovitch Prize, the Victor Lynch Staunton Award, and the Governor General's Playwrights Award, to name but a few. Newfoundland theatre continues to be interactive, cooperative, strong and vibrant.

Film: St. John's has become a film production centre as demon- strated by the films *Rare Birds, Grown Up Movie Star, The Red Door, Random Passage, Misery Harbour, Secret Nation* and *The Adventure of Faustus Bidgood.* CBC's production of the *Republic of Doyle*, which began in 2008, is set in St. John's and can be seen filming in the city and surrounding areas. The series is viewed nationally and internationally. Many local independent filmmakers operate in Newfoundland and Labrador and are promoted by NIFCO, one of the most successful and productive film cooperatives in the country.

Newfoundland Symphony Orchestra: The St. John's Symphony Orchestra started in the late 1960s and performed three concerts a year by 1970. Peter Gardner was engaged as concertmaster in 1971, the first full-time professional musician. The Newfoundland Symphony Orchestra (NSO) was incorporated in 1979 and branched into the Atlantic String Quartet, the Newfoundland Symphony Youth Orchestra, the Philharmonic Choir of the NSO, the Sinfonia, the Newfoundland Symphony Youth Choir and the NSO Light Orchestra.

The School of Music at Memorial University of Newfoundland: Outstanding musicians are produced at the Music School. Concerts are held in the acoustically rich 296-seat Donald F. Cook Recital Hall. A recently updated **History of Music Display** in the Recital Hall lobby exhibits historical photographs, printed programs and sheet music covers from 1870 to the present. **The Music Resource Centre** is a library-run collection of published research materials and scores in the Morgan Building. **The Research Centre for the Study of Music Media and Place (MMaP)**, at the Arts and Culture Centre, specializes in original ethnographic research and digitization of traditional recordings to preserve the past and allow the public greater access to the rich traditional music of the province.

Festivals

ST. JOHN'S TIME

Four festivals that occur within a two-week period in late July-early August: **Newfoundland & Labrador Folk Festival** is held on an outdoor stage in Bannerman Park and features musicians, dancers and storytellers from around the province and "away." A great chance to experience Newfoundland traditional music; **George Street Festival** is the ultimate summer festival on St. John's most famous street; **Royal St. John's Regatta** (see page 69); **Downtown Buskers' Festival** where local, national and international entertainers perform on three stages in downtown St. John's.

OTHER FESTIVALS

Sound Symposium is an international festival of new music, sound, audio, acoustic and performing art held in St. John's bi-annually and gathers musicians, filmmakers, actors, dancers, and visual, multi-media and environmental artists, local and international; **Festival 500 Sharing the Voices** is a celebrated international non-competitive festival of choral music held on alternate years with the Sound Symposium; the city sponsors free lunch-time concerts at the **Harbourside Park** in the summer; **Nickel Independent Film Festival** is an international festival for filmmakers. All screenings are held at the LSPU Hall, with outdoor screenings also held downtown in the summer; **Opera on the Avalon** is an international festival for emerging operatic artists; **Mardi Gras Halloween Party** is held on George Street at the end of October; **Wreckhouse International Jazz and Blues** promotes the enjoyment and appreciation of jazz, blues and world music in Newfoundland and Labrador; **St. John's Storytelling Festival** is an international festival promoting the art and tradition of storytelling; **St. John's Comedy Festival; Women's International Film Festival; Shakespeare by the Sea** is the longest running outdoor summer theatre event in St. John's; **Festival of New Dance** brings together the best and most innovative dancers in Newfoundland and Labrador and across Canada; **Mummers Festival.**

chapter five

SURROUNDED BY WATER

Newfoundland is the sixteenth largest island in the world. Its land area is 111,390 sq km (43,008 sq miles), and about one eighth of its area is water. There are approximately 29,000 km (18,020 miles) of coastline. The land area of Labrador is 294,330 sq km (113,642 sq miles). The total land area of Newfoundland and Labrador is 405,720 sq km (156,650 sq miles) — more than three times the total area of Nova Scotia, New Brunswick and Prince Edward Island and almost one and three quarters times the size of Great Britain.

Newfoundland is situated in the Gulf of St. Lawrence at the "gateway to Canada." It lies between the 46th and 61st parallels. St. John's is on the same latitude as Paris, France, but its weather leads one to believe that it is farther north.

THE NEWFOUNDLAND CLIMATE

The meeting of two ocean currents determines the island's climate. The Labrador Current, flowing from the Arctic to Newfoundland via Labrador, and the Gulf Stream, flowing in a northerly direction from the Equator to eastern North America, meet off the south coast of Newfoundland. The warm current meeting the cold Arctic current produces a cooling effect and usually fog, the cause of many shipwrecks and great loss of life in the past. Nowadays radar is essential for ships and fishing boats in this area with some of the worst fogs in the world.

Newfoundland is famous for its unsettled weather. The wind can change at will, and it is said that four seasons can occur in one day. The climate is temperate, cooled in summer and moderated in winter by winds, with rare weather below -18 C (0 F). The annual rainfall in St. John's is about 158 cm (62 inches). The average yearly temperature recorded is around 5 C (40 F) with a high of 30 C (86 F) and a low of -23 C (-10 F). There is snow from January to about April. Spring is almost nonexistent with summer suddenly arriving in May or June. Drift ice occasionally fills St. John's harbour during March, April and May. This has happened twice since 1949 to the point that the harbour could not be used for navigation.

THE GRAND BANKS

The Grand Banks, on the continental shelf off Newfoundland, consist of approximately 155,400 sq km (60,000 sq miles), with less than 100 fathoms (600 feet) of depth in the water. Due to the meeting of the Labrador Current and the Gulf Stream, the area is rich in plankton — a rich food for fish. The area around Lily and Carson Canyons on the fringe of the Banks is one of the most lucrative fishing areas.

The wreck of R.M.S. *Titanic* was discovered off the Grand Banks in 1985 by Dr. Robert Ballard of the Woods Hole Oceanographic Institution in more than 12,800 feet (3,900 m) of water. The *Titanic* had sunk almost 73 years earlier in 1912.

"The *Titanic* lies in 13,000 feet of water on a gently sloping alpine-like countryside overlooking a small canyon below. Its bow faces north and the ship sits upright on the bottom. There is no light at this great depth and little life can be found. It is a quiet and peaceful and fitting place for the remains of this

greatest sea tragedy to rest. May it ever remain this way
and may God bless these found souls."
                    – Dr. Robert Ballard, September 9, 1985

NEWFOUNDLAND'S EARLY FISHERY

Newfoundland was discovered by Europeans at a time when
many countries wanted fish, an important source of protein. At
the time, the sea was reported to be swarming with so many fish
they could not only be taken in nets, but in baskets let down with
a stone. John Cabot, in 1497, is said to have described the cod as
being so thick they slowed down the progress of his ship.

In those early years, the fishing season and voyage to and from
the banks kept early European fishermen away from home for
lengthy periods. The two main types of fishery were the wet or
green fishery and the dry fishery. The green fishermen cleaned
and salted the caught fish right on board the ships. When they
returned home, the fish, still in its wet or green condition,
was then washed, dried and salted. The French, Portuguese and
Spanish traditionally used this method. It was not necessary to
come ashore as often as the dry fishermen, who had to build
stages and flakes on shore to clean and cure the catch.

Fishermen came in sailing ships and caught fish by hand over the
side until about the 20th century. Handlining was difficult and
labour-intensive work. Fishermen often stood in barrels tied to
the deck of the ship, for protection and support from the wind
and weather. Each fisherman had a pair of handlines about
100 metres (328 ft) long with one or two hooks, and a weight.
The entire line had to be hauled up when a fish was hooked. Fifty
quintals, or five thousand pounds of fish, was a man's work for
the summer.

A more efficient method of fishing was adopted in the 1850s
when the fishermen went from their ships in small dories and set
trawls or longlines with hundreds of hooks. The crew was able to
fish a much larger area. A dory is a flat-bottomed boat developed

for the inshore fishery. It was ideal for the bank fishery as it could be stacked on the decks of a schooner to save space. It was also very seaworthy and could carry large loads of fish.

Fishing was the main source of income for Newfoundland settlers, and the inshore fishing ground became overcrowded. Small schooners brought the colonial fishermen to the offshore banks. The catch could be lightly salted as they were not far from home. On return to port the fish were unloaded from the ship's hold with fish forks, washed to remove dirt and excess salt, and then piled to press out excess moisture. The catch was then spread on large flakes to dry in the sun. When partially dry the fish were piled again to press out more moisture. This was repeated until the catch was properly preserved. The fish were sorted by size and quality and packed in barrels or stored in bulk. Bulk fish were dried again in the sun before being exported.

Fishing for cod in a dory. From steel engraving in *The Graphic*, October 17, 1891
COURTESY LEOFRAMES ANTIQUES PRINTS BRIGHTON

COD FISH

Cod was an important food staple in the days before refrigeration. The flesh could be preserved either by drying or by salting. Dried cod kept well and was less expensive than meat. Consequently it gained a wide market in hot countries, especially amongst the poor. Atlantic cod has been one of the major fish resources of Canada, and "fish" in Newfoundland always meant cod fish. The **northern cod stock**, inhabiting the area from mid Labrador to the Grand Banks has supplied about three quarters of all the fish landed in Newfoundland and Labrador. Today, the stock is in serious trouble and fishermen are looking to other species.

Fisheries managers study the habits and features of different stocks – their migration, spawning, growth patterns and life span. Tagging is one method of studying fish movement. Scientists then rely on fishermen to return any tags found on fish caught. Each tag supplies information on where and when the fish was tagged and where and when it was caught, helping to build up a picture of the movement of different fish stocks. Cod in southerly waters grow faster than the same species living in colder waters farther north. A few fish stray far from their home waters. A cod tagged off northern Europe in 1957 was caught off Newfoundland, more than 2,000 miles (3,220 km) away, in 1961.

Cod spawn offshore in winter and spring, normally in deep water, and spawning information is known only from behaviour studied in tanks. Northerly cod tend to spawn earlier than those farther south, perhaps due to slower development in colder waters. After spawning, the eggs gradually rise to the surface and drift with the current. How many survive at this stage depends largely on where the current takes them. Cod lay millions of eggs, but only a few from each pair survive. Each cod that reaches maturity, escaping all the dangers in its existence, is truly one in a million.

THE SCHOONER

A sailing vessel is referred to by her rigging, which defines an arrangement of masts, spars, yards and sails. A schooner is described as a ship having two gaff sails, the fore being larger than the after sail, and a head sail. The two-masted schooner was developed in New England around 1700. The fore and aft sails could be manipulated from the deck, making schooners more manageable than square-rigged vessels. The early schooners were only about 60 feet (18.3 m) long and had a crew of ten or twelve. The original vessels on the American coast were called catches and shallops. The name schooner appeared early in the 18th century, coming about by the peculiar skipping motion, or "scooning," made by the smaller sailing vessels.

The influence of schooners developed in the American colonies during this period spread northwards into Nova Scotia, New Brunswick, Prince Edward Island, Newfoundland and Labrador. The schooner needed only a small crew in proportion to its size, and was ideal for the westerly prevailing winds along the east coast of North America. It was also made popular by its ability at sea during the winter. Frost and ice made navigation difficult and the crew was able to do all their work on deck in the freezing weather, instead of aloft as was necessary on the larger ships.

The "Fisherman" schooner, introduced in 1900 by a Boston yacht designer, Mr. B.B. Crowninshield, had short, straight keels, raking stern posts, long overhanging counters and a cut away forefoot. These changes formed a break at the forward end of the keel and a curved sweep to the stem head. The Fisherman profile included a full two-masted schooner rig with a bowsprit, similar to that of the famous *Bluenose*, and was widely used in Newfoundland.

There was an ongoing tradition of boat building in Newfoundland, with its roots in its British ancestry, which in many areas developed into an industry. The tradition was passed from father to son in an informal manner. New designs such as the Western or Jack Schooner, Bully Boat, Fisherman and Banking Schooner gradually became adapted to suit Newfoundland conditions.

Most transportation and travel in Newfoundland between the far-flung coastal communities was by schooner. The sea was the principal highway for most Newfoundland outports. Coastal boats and schooners moved passengers and freight in the only possible way among the scattered coves and villages along the vast coastline. Most people lived close to the sea, depended on the sea for a livelihood and relied on boats as their only link to the outside world. Boats were indispensable elements of fishing, transportation, communication and commerce.

Sailing schooner *Norma and Gladys*
COURTESY MARITIME HISTORY ACHIVE

LIFE IN A FISHING SCHOONER

The fishing season opened in March and continued until October. Most vessels made about two or three trips to the banks during that period. Each trip was about three weeks but could be as long as eight weeks if the fishing was poor. The schooner had a small forward cabin, where most of the men slept, cooked and ate. The captain and a few of the men lived in an aft cabin. The two fish holds took up most of the space on the boat. The provisions were kept in the bilges below the galley to keep cool. Long hours of hard work were part of life at sea, work starting before daylight and continuing until late at night. There was a cycle of baiting, fishing, bringing the fish on board and cleaning and storing it in the hold. Men were often lost in the fog in their dories; sometimes they were recovered but often were not. It was said that two standard traditions for most fishermen were that it was unlucky to work on Sunday and useless for a fisherman to learn to swim as he would not be able to survive far from land in the cold Atlantic waters. Another saying was that a man who would go to sea for a living would go to hell for a pastime. Many suffered badly from the elements but knew no other way of life. The Grand Bank fishery was one of great hazards, long distances and lengths of time away from home. Tragedy often struck with fog or storms separating dories and men from their ships.

TRADITIONAL FISHING GEAR IN NEWFOUNDLAND

Jigger: The traditional jigger is lead and the Norwegian jigger is made of stainless steel. No bait is needed; the jigger is lowered almost to the bottom and then drawn up and down. Cod are lured and may be caught by the head, body or tail. The new regulations allow only a single hook on the jigger.

Handline: The hook is usually baited with squid. A series of hooks with artificial bait is sometimes also attached to the line. A heavy lead weight is used to keep the bait near the bottom. Fishermen frequently had a line on each side of the boat.

Trawls or Long Lines: Trawls have many short lines attached at regular intervals. Each short line has a hook which is usually baited with squid. Trawls are placed on the bottom with a small anchor at each end and marked by buoys. They are hauled to the boat to remove the fish and usually coiled in tubs to be rebaited ashore. Each line is 50 fathoms long (350 ft) and 20 to 30 lines are often set together. (There are six feet in a fathom. It is used to measure depth of water.)

Deep-Sea Trawls: Introduced in the 1930s, deep-sea trawls are very large net bags lowered into the water from the back of stern trawlers and the sides of side trawlers. The ships are connected to the nets by two cables — one from each side of the opening of the bag which is hauled along behind the trawler gathering everything in its path. The trawl is hauled on board, emptied of its catch and returned to the water.

Salmon Nets are made of nylon with many small floats along the top and with a lead foot rope. The net is kept on the surface with large buoys and held in place by heavy anchors. Salmon are caught by their gills and removed without taking the net from the water. Nets are usually 50 fathoms long. The new regulations do not allow net fishing.

Gill Nets are similar in construction to salmon nets. They are made of monofilament and sunk to the bottom by small weights. The ends are marked by buoys. The nets are hauled into the boats to remove the fish and then reset in the water. Three or four nets are often set together. Nets are 50 fathoms long and one fathom deep. The new regulations do not allow net fishing.

A Cod Trap is like a mesh box with a floor resting on the bottom. The top is held up by many small floats and large buoys from the corners, sides and back. Each of these is secured by a heavy anchor. The cod fish are diverted into the door of the trap, as they follow capelin, by the leader which projects from the door towards the shore. The size and shape of traps vary, the average being 60 fathoms around and with a 50-fathom leader. They are usually hauled twice a day by a crew working from a trap boat aided by a dory. First the door is closed by hauling up a rope attached to the bottom front. Then the front corners are hauled up and the fish are gradually collected along one side or the back by hauling in the mesh bottom. The catch is taken into the boat by a dip net.

Cod Pots are being introduced in the inshore fishery. They are similar to cod traps but are baited, catch fewer fish that are brought up alive and bled at sea, which produces a very high quality product. The cod pot fishery is quite limited at present, with hopes for expansion in the future.

SPECIES FISHERY

Crab Fishery: Crab contributes significantly to Newfoundland's once cod-dependent economy. Queen crab or "snow crab" was once considered a nuisance species by Newfoundland fishermen. They began to be fished commercially in 1969 with dramatic increases in landings since then. Crab boats range from around 20 feet (6.1 m) to a maximum of 65 feet (20 m) and carry a five or six man crew. Crab are caught in baited conical crab pots, 48 in. (122 cm) in diameter at the bottom, 28 in. (71 cm) at the top and 24 in. (61 cm) high. The pot is emptied into the boat hold and the crab sorted for size into boxes. The pots are rebaited and set again in "fleets" in the water. Female and undersized crab are returned to the ocean. At the end of a two or three day trip the chilled boxed crab are graded live on the wharf for quality and taken to a plant for processing.

The **Shrimp Fishery** is a trawl fishery using towed shrimp trawls. Shrimp are caught in bottom trawls similar to those used for groundfish. Bycatch reduction devices on the nets are mandatory to prevent the number of other species caught in the trawls. The shrimp are placed in the hold and taken to plants for processing. Larger vessels cook and package the shrimp while at sea.

Surf Clams or ocean quahogs are fished on the Grand Banks by Clearwater Seafoods Limited of Nova Scotia and processed in plants at Grand Bank on the south coast of Newfoundland.

Turbot or Greenland halibut are fished using gill nets; 25 to 60 nets are joined together to make up a "fleet." The two to three miles of net go to the bottom and start fishing. They are hauled within two to three days and the fish picked out of the nets by hand — this process can take up to 24 hours. The fish are cleaned, washed and iced before being off loaded at a fish plant for processing.

Capelin are most abundantly found in Canada in areas around Newfoundland and Labrador. Most live on banks offshore and spawn on beaches or gravel shoals near shore. Spawning takes place in June and July when mature capelin move towards the beaches. Females usually release all of their eggs at one time, an average of 4600. Males may mate more than once but most female capelin die after spawning. The eggs stick to sand or gravel and hatch in 15 to 20 days. The larvae stay in the gravel

Casting for capelin, circa 1920
MARY SOUTHCOTT PHOTOGRAPH, COURTESY DR. N. RUSTED

ST. JOHN'S : A BRIEF HISTORY

Fishing for capelin, circa 1920
MARY SOUTHCOTT PHOTOGRAPH, COURTESY DR. N. RUSTED

until washed out by the waves, return to offshore banks to feed on plankton and take three or four years to mature.

Newfoundland's commercial capelin fishery supplies roe-bearing female fish to Japan. The catch is valuable and therefore an important commercial species. Capelin are also an important forage fish in the northwest Atlantic, fed upon by seabirds, seals, whales, haddock, flounder, salmon, herring and, most of all, by cod.

The "capelin scull" usually takes place in late June or early July. Schools of spawning capelin are driven into shallow water by cod fish and ashore by the tides. It is said locally that the capelin are

rolling ashore. Each year Newfoundlanders look forward to the capelin run and go to the beaches to watch the activity, catch capelin to eat or to use as fertilizer in their gardens. The capelin are handpicked from the beach or caught in cast nets.

Seal Fishery: The Hooded, Ringed, Harp, Gray, Bearded and Harbour seals live in Newfoundland and Labrador. Harp seals spend the summer in the Arctic and migrate to Newfoundland waters in late fall, giving birth to their pups on the pack ice in the early spring. They gather in large concentrations to shed their fur east of Belle Isle, and then move back north.

Sealing was a traditional part of Newfoundland's economy, at first for the seal oil, then for pelts for leather and fur, and the meat. Sealing helped diversify the economy and encourage permanent settlement. Much of northern Newfoundland was populated in areas such as Fogo, Greenspond and Bonavista because of sealing in the spring, trapping fur, fishing salmon in the early summer and the summer fishery.

Sealing was part of the scene in St. John's in the 19th and early 20th centuries. The first ships sailed to the ice from St. John's in 1795. The hunt expanded rapidly and after 1800 over 100 small vessels carried between 3500 and 4000 men to the ice each spring. Many spin-off industries developed from the hunt. Seal oil factories were located on the south side of St. John's harbour. The northern seal hunt took place annually in March and April when hundreds of men flocked to St. John's to get a "berth" on one of the sealing ships to the "front" — the breeding ground of the harp and hooded seals located on the pack ice off northern Newfoundland and southeastern Labrador. The harbour in St. John's would be crowded with people watching the blessing of the fleet and its departure with great fanfare and sirens blowing.

Sealing ships in St. John's harbour
MARITIME HISTORY ARCHIVE

The seal hunt is a dangerous occupation and many men were lost, frozen to death or crippled, and vessels lost at sea or on the ice. Newfoundland's sealing tradition and hunt was almost lost in 1970 when international animal welfare groups won their protest against the hunt.

Today, the government of Canada has issued statements:

"... in support of the importance of the sealing industry for people and individuals for their livelihood; and for the economies of coastal communities. The freeze on personal use licenses has been lifted for residents living near sealing areas, allowing up to 6 per person. The hunt is an economic mainstay for many rural communities and supports many families who can gain as much as 35% of their annual income from this activity."

The Total Allowable Catch (TAC) has trebled since the 1970s and 70% has been allocated to waters east of Newfoundland and Labrador. Commercial licenses are limited and the harvest is rigorously monitored to comply with regulations and license conditions. A training and certification program is being developed and offered to current and future license holders.

NEWFOUNDLAND SEA LIFE AND SEABIRDS

Basking sharks are quite common in Newfoundland. They are the second largest fish in the world, not dangerous but sometimes harmful to inshore fishermen when they collide with nets. Much of the damage to inshore fishing gear by basking sharks is blamed on whales. The sharks' dorsal and tail fins are brownish coloured and can be seen where the basking sharks "bask" on the surface of the water on calm days. Adults range from 20-30 feet (6.1-9.1 m) and have very rough skin, baleen which strain plankton and food from the water, and tiny teeth. Basking sharks are distinguished from other common sharks in Newfoundland waters by their large size, baleen, and huge gill arches. They look a little like whales on the surface, but whales move more quickly than basking sharks, breathe on the surface and are warm blooded. Basking sharks' brains are the size of golf balls, while that of the whale is larger than a human's. The basking shark swims along with its mouth open to feed, straining plankton from the water with its baleen. It hibernates on the bottom in winter due to the low plankton abundance at this time.

Whales: There about 20 different species of whales in Newfoundland. Whales are mammals, breathe air, produce their young alive, nurse them on milk, and have developed to survive entirely in water. Whale watching is an exciting experience and is possible in the St. John's area during the months of June to August from Signal Hill, Cape Spear and on some of the boat tours departing from the St. John's harbour and Bay Bulls, on the Southern Shore. Whales can be identified by their size, dorsal fins, and the shape of their blow when they come up for air, or, as in the case of the humpback whale, its flukes when it dives.

Humpback Whales: Most humpback whales are seen from May to September, but most commonly in the summer months when food is more plentiful. They range in length from 35-40 feet (10-13 m), the young from 25 feet (7.6 m) and the female 3-4 feet (0.9-1.2 m) longer than the male. Humpbacks are noted for their long white flippers, which are about one third of their body length, and wart-like knobs on their heads. Their blow is a bushy balloon shape; the back is usually then seen. After about five to ten blows, a final dive is often seen, with tail flukes seen clearly above the water. Fluke patterns on the tail are used to identify individual animals, like fingerprints in humans.

Spectacular acrobatics are associated with the humpback. They can leap into the air, lie on their sides and roll, waving and slapping their flippers into the air and water. They also can raise their tails into the air and repeatedly slap the water. These behaviours make the humpback a thrilling animal to watch.

Fin Whales are commonly seen from early spring until late fall, and travel in groups of two to eight. The blow is long and column shaped, and there may be five to eight blows before the whale dives again. Unlike the humpback, the fin whale does not show its flukes when beginning a dive.

Minke Whales: The minke is a common whale in Newfoundland and Labrador during the summer and fall. It is seen mostly on its own and usually close to shore, but may be found farther out and in small groups. The whales are black on top with white bellies. Their blows are close to the surface and difficult to see.

Pilot (Pothead) Whales: The "pothead" comes to Newfoundland and Labrador waters during late summer and early fall in search of squid and fish. It is black with a long curved dorsal fin. The pothead gets its name from its pot-shaped head.

Seabirds: The Newfoundland coastline is home to many species of seabirds: puffins, gannets, black-legged kittiwakes, Atlantic turres, storm petrels, northern razorbills, cormorants, southern black guillemots and herring gulls. Several of the more than 400 puffin colonies in Newfoundland are the largest on the continent of North America, and the three gannet colonies amongst the second largest. Boat tours out of St. John's and Bay Bulls, on the Southern Shore, view many of these birds in their natural environment. Thousands can be seen soaring in the air or perched on the rugged cliffs. You will be amazed by the sight and sounds. A day trip to Cape St. Mary's Ecological Reserve (usually referred to as the bird sanctuary) is a splendid outing to see seabirds. Bird Rock is the second largest nesting place for gannets in North America. The sanctuaries provide great photographic opportunities.

Chapter six

THE COLLAPSE
OF THE RESOURCE BASE

There was unrestricted 12-month fishing in Newfoundland and Labrador waters during the late 1950s and 1960s. The big declines in the fish stocks were almost entirely due to foreign overfishing as well as trawlers and factory trawlers that salted or iced fish at sea. This period was the beginning of a long-term decline that never recovered from the devastation to the fish stocks. Historically, the catch was sustainable at approximately 400,000 tons per annum. The key was to keep harvest levels low so the fish can sustain themselves, but this did not happen. The summer fishery northern cod catch was 200,000 to 300,000 tons. The government reported that the 1968 foreign fishery northern cod catch was 810,000 tons and the total catch was almost 1.2 million tons for all cod stocks.

The Harris Report recommendations of the Independent Review Panel on Northern Cod, released in 1990, stated that "Northern cod stocks have been exploited by fishermen since c.1481. Although these patterns have varied, these stocks were, for at least four hundred years, the economic foundation for growth of a settled community along the east and northeast coasts of Newfoundland and the coast of Labrador. Though supplemented by comparatively modest contributions from other marine species such as salmon, herring, seals and whales, the cod stocks were the raison d'être for the existence of Newfoundland as a colony."

The fishery had been the basis of Newfoundland's economy for centuries and the resource base of the fishery — the northern cod stocks on the Grand Banks — essentially collapsed. The moratorium, or closure of commercial fishing, was established on July 2, 1992, by the Government of Canada. The moratorium had major consequences of a social, political and economic nature. It had a drastic effect on the economy, causing great uncertainty about the future and affecting the lives of thousands of people. Many lost their only means of livelihood. It caused a loss of employment and income for 12,000 fishermen and 15,000 plant workers, as well as 1,200 others affected by the impact upon Fishery Products International and other large operations.

NCARP, the Northern Cod Adjustment and Recovery Program, and AGAP, the Atlantic Groundfish Adjustment Program, were implemented as income assistance to aid fishermen and plant workers until May 14, 1994. TAGS, The Atlantic Groundfish Strategy, replaced NCARP and AGAP on May 16, 1994. These programs were designed to decrease dependence on the fishery but were not the solution to the problem.

Many things contributed to the decline of the northern cod stocks and resulting moratorium.

❖ Overfishing in the 1960s was almost all foreign based.

❖ The 200-mile limit in 1977 created an eager rush to the fishery and major capital investment. The industry expanded much too quickly and kept up until it was stopped by the economic crisis.

❖ Fish stocks started to decline in the 1960s. Rapid ocean cooling between 1982-1985 affected cod spawning and development of the young. It was only apparent in the later years that most species were affected, especially cod off Labrador. The lack of young fish was not apparent until it was too late. This serious problem resulted in the 1992 Moratorium.

❖ Spain and Portugal joined the European Economic Community in 1985. One of the EEC stipulations was that they were not to fish in EEC waters until six years later. The EEC asked NAFO (Northwest Atlantic Fisheries Organization) for bigger quotas but was refused by the Canadian Government. The EEC objected. This resulted in unrestrained fishing by Spain, Portugal and several other EEC countries outside the 200-mile limit at a time when cod stocks were in decline.

❖ The ocean-ecosystem cooling off Labrador in the years 1985-89 resulted in cod and other species migrating south. The northern cod off Newfoundland were concentrated on the east coast and overfished by the EEC both before and after the moratorium and especially during the declines of the early 1990s. The northern cod stocks have not recovered to date.

The Newfoundland and Labrador ocean ecosystem changed significantly during the 1980s and 1990s. Cod stocks declined to low levels, and in contrast snow crab and northern shrimp levels have increased and become the most important fisheries in the province.

To date, there has been little recovery in the northern cod stocks. Canada has a goal of keeping three fishery patrol vessels on the edge of the Grand Banks year round. Custodial management has been advanced by some federal and provincial politicians, an idea that has been closely examined by the Advisory Panel on Straddling Stocks (those on the edge of the Grand Banks) and found to have no basis in international law.

THE PRESENT FISHERY

The moratorium on the cod fishery affects Labrador and the northeast coast to Cape St. Mary's, but *not* the south or west coasts where the fisheries were not and are not based on the northern cod. There is a continuing small scale "monitoring" cod fishery on the northeast coast, big enough to supply the local market, including restaurants, which usually have cod on the menu, which can be very confusing to anyone who has heard that the cod fishery is no more.

The worldwide demand for seafood is still there and we need to go forward. Newfoundland's important fisheries are crab, shrimp, lobster, cod and capelin. Next in importance are plaice, yellowtail flounder, halibut, turbot, redfish, mackerel, and a variety of minor species such as haddock, greysole, monkfish and skate. Seals are also on the list as a "fishery."

Derek Butler, Executive Director of the Newfoundland and Labrador Seafood Producers, listed the most valuable 2009 species in landed value in declining order:

- Snow crab $149 million
- Shrimp $109 million
- Surf clams $45 million
- Turbot $20 million
- Cod $15 million

The top 2008 species in declining order were:

- Snow Crab $179 million
- Shrimp $178 million
- Surf clams $28 million
- Cod $28 million
- Lobster $28 million
- Turbot $17 million

Aquaculture: Newfoundland and Labrador's clear, clean water is ideally suited for aquaculture as long as the area is ice free, i.e., the south coast. It is experimental at the moment and the focus is mainly on Atlantic salmon, steelhead trout, blue mussels and Atlantic Cod.

SOCIAL IMPLICATIONS OF THE DOWNTURN IN THE FISHERY

Newfoundland's demographic is changing quickly. St. John's has new professional and skilled people moving in to work mainly in the oil and gas industry. Rural Newfoundland presently has the lowest birth rate of any province or state in North America. Fewer and older people still live scattered in small communities, which offers huge challenges for education, medicine, transportation and electrical service.

The fishery can be lucrative but cannot support people in rural Newfoundland. The workers in the processing sector are getting older. Young people are not as attracted to these seasonal jobs as they were in the past. They are becoming better educated and leaving the island for greater opportunities elsewhere; 20- to 30-year-olds tend to go and stay away whereas 40- to 50-year-olds often go and come back, only to leave again.

Well-paying professional and non-professional jobs are available in such places as Fort McMurray, Alberta. Many workers live in Newfoundland but travel to their jobs, spending six weeks there and then a month home, and variations on that schedule. Rural Newfoundland is prosperous as never before. You can go almost anywhere and see new and renovated houses, huge pickup trucks and attractive, well-kept properties.

Government controls and regulation to protect the fish stocks have increased paperwork and red tape for the fishermen. One fisherman commented, "The fishery is a good living, but regulations make me wonder if I should give it up … it's stressful, you almost need someone on shore to handle all the regulations, conditions, fees and licenses."

A worldwide phenomenon also affects Newfoundland processing plants. Some factory trawlers gut fish, freeze it at sea and send it to China where it is thawed, processed very cheaply, and the products sent around the world — even into our own supermarkets. Canadian processors cannot compete with these products because of our higher labour costs. The **Professional Fish Harvesters** Certification Board (PFHCB) is advancing professional development of the fishery through registration, certification and accreditation to "ensure fishermen have the skills and knowledge required to succeed in the demanding and rapidly changing industry, to bestow professional status on those with long term attachment and set qualifying standards for new entrants."

chapter seven

LOOKING TO THE FUTURE

The vast oil fields of Hibernia, Terra Nova and White Rose, located on the Grand Banks off St John's, produce almost half of Canada's conventional light crude oil. St. John's has emerged as the primary business centre for east coast oil exploration, development and production. The offshore energy industry presently injects more than $770 million into the local economy and future opportunities exist with exploration in the Orphan Basin and Laurentian Sub-basin.

OFFSHORE DEVELOPMENT

Hibernia: Oil and gas were discovered on the Grand Banks in 1979, and a Binding Agreement was signed September 14, 1990. The Hibernia oil field, named for the ship, the S.S. *Hibernia,* which helped lay communications cable between Heart's Content, Newfoundland, and Ireland in the 1800s, is located 315 km (196 miles) off the coast of Newfoundland on the eastern edge of the Grand Banks in 80 m (263 ft) of water.

The Hibernia offshore oil field is owned jointly by ExxonMobil Canada (33.125%), Chevron Canada Resources (26.875%), Petro-Canada (20%), Canada Hibernia Holding Corporation (8.5%), Murphy Oil (6.5%) and Statoil Canada Ltd. (5%).

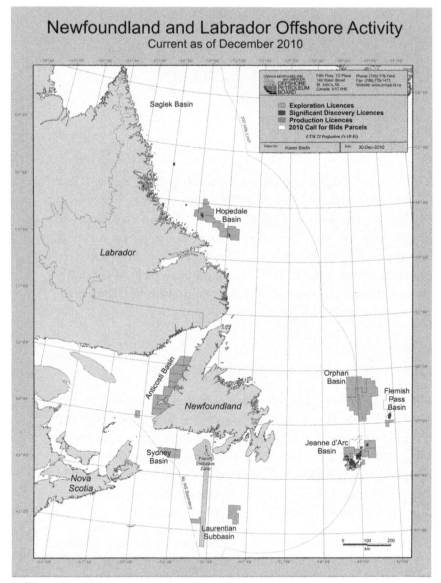

Newfoundland and Labrador Offshore Activity
Current as of December 2010

Saglek Basin

CANADA-NEWFOUNDLAND
and LABRADOR
OFFSHORE
PETROLEUM
BOARD

Fifth Floor, TD Place
140 Water Street
St. John's, NL
Canada A1C 6H6

Phone: (709) 778-1400
Fax: (709) 778-1473
Website: www.cnlopb.nl.ca

Exploration Licences
Significant Discovery Licences
Production Licences
2010 Call for Bids Parcels

UTM 22 Projection (NAD 83)

Karen Smith   30-Dec-2010

Hopedale
Basin

Labrador

Anticosti Basin

Orphan
Basin

Flemish
Pass
Basin

Newfoundland

French
Exclusive
Zone

NL-NS Boundary

Sydney
Basin

Jeanne d'Arc
Basin

Nova
Scotia

Laurentian
Subbasin

0   100   200
km

Offshore development areas

The Hibernia oil production facility includes a concrete pedestal or Gravity Base Structure (GBS), the Topsides oil production facilities, a crude oil loading system, and two purpose-built shuttle tankers. Two production reservoirs are located in the Hibernia oil field: the Hibernia sandstones and the Avalon sandstones.

The Topsides facilities accommodate all drilling, producing and utility equipment on the Hibernia platform, and provide living quarters for the steady-state crew of approximately 220 people. The Topsides facilities have a design capacity of approximately 230,000 barrels of crude oil production per day. In 2003, the Canada-Newfoundland and Labrador Offshore Petroleum Board (C-NLOPB) gave Hibernia permission to increase its annual production rate to 220,000 barrels per day.

The Gravity Base Structure was used in the North Sea, an environment similar to Newfoundland. The construction site of the GBS and the assembly of completed topsides was Mosquito Cove in Bull Arm, Trinity Bay, on the northeast coast of Newfoundland, 130 km (81 miles) northwest of St. John's. Construction began at Bull Arm in October 1990.

The Bull Arm Fabrication Site is a world-class fabrication facility with capabilities for steel fabrication and concrete construction, outfitting installation, at-shore hook-up and commissioning. It has an ice-free port, marine facilities and adjacent deep water, allowing for near-shore mating and hook-up. Major fabrication, industrial or manufacturing projects can be performed from start to finish at this one location with access to the worldwide marine transportation network. The 4,000-acre construction site is a small, fully serviced town for more than 3,400 people.

The 120,000-ton GBS was towed on November 14, 1994, from the dry dock area to the deep-water construction site where the second phase of construction took place. The completed platform was towed to the Hibernia oil field and positioned on the ocean floor in June 1997 and began producing oil on November 17, 1997. The platform stands 224 m (735 ft) high, half the height of

New York's Empire State Building (449 m, 1,473 ft) and 33 m (108 ft) taller than the Calgary Tower (191 m, 627 ft).

White Rose Development: The White Rose oil field project is located 350 km (217.5 miles) off the coast of Newfoundland in the Jeanne d'Arc Basin. Husky Energy is the operator and 72.5% interest holder in the White Rose oil fields, with Suncor Energy holding a 27.5% interest.

Discovered in 1984, the field consists of both oil and gas pools, including the South White Rose oil pool. The oil pool covers approximately 40 square km and contains an estimated 440 million barrels of recoverable oil. White Rose is the second harsh environment development in North America to use a Floating Production Storage and Offloading (FPSO) vessel, the *Sea Rose* FPSO. Production from the field began November 12, 2005.

Terra Nova Oil Field: The Terra Nova oil field development project is located 350 km (217.5 miles) off the coast of New-foundland. Discovered in 1984 by Petro-Canada, the field is the second largest off Canada's east coast. Terra Nova is the first harsh environment development in North America to use a Floating Production Storage and Offloading (FPSO) vessel, the *Terra Nova* FPSO. Production from the field began in January 2002.

The oil is produced from the Late Jurassic-aged sandstone within the Jeanne d'Arc Formation. The reservoir was deposited as a large, braided fluvial system.

The partners are Suncor Energy (33.99% – operator), Exxon-Mobil Canada Properties (22%), Statoil (15%), Husky Energy Operations Ltd. (12.51%), Murphy Oil Company Ltd. (12%), Mosbacher Operating Ltd. (3.5%) and Chevron Canada Resources (1%).

Hebron Project: Hebron is located in the Jeanne d'Arc Basin, 350 km (217.5 miles) southeast of St John's. The Hebron co-venturers signed the final agreement with the province on August 20, 2008. The development of the Hebron oil field will be the fourth stand-alone offshore oil project.

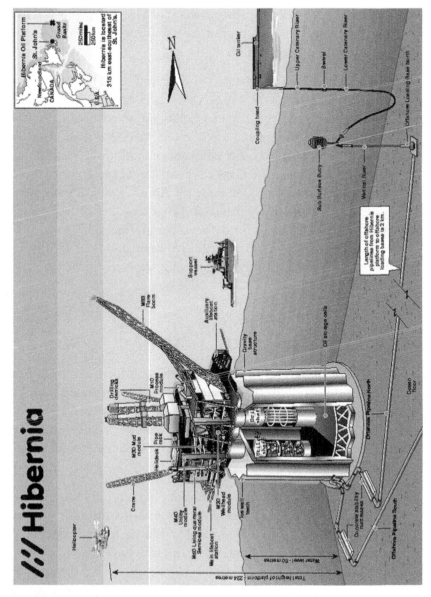

Schematic of Hibernia Gravity Based Structure Production Platform and Oil Loading System to shuttle tankers

The Hebron field is located 9 km north of the Terra Nova project, 32 km (20 miles) southeast of the Hibernia project, and 46 km (28.6 miles) southeast of the White Rose project.

The project owners are ExxonMobil Canada Properties (36%), Chevron Canada Resources (26.7%), Suncor Energy (22.7%) and Statoil Canada (9.7%). Nalcor Energy, owned by the province, has purchased a 4.9% equity share at a cost of $110 million. It will pay a proportional share of project costs and receive a proportional share of project production.

The Hebron field is estimated to contain 585 million barrels of recoverable reserves. It will be developed using a conventional drilling and production topsides facility mounted atop a concrete GBS. Construction of the topsides and GBS is due to begin in 2012 at Bull Arm and other fabrication locations in Newfoundland and Labrador. The GBS base will contain storage for more than one million barrels of crude oil. An offshore loading system (OLS) with a looped pipeline and two separate loading points will be installed to offload the oil from the GBS onto ice-strengthened tankers for transfer to a transhipment facility or transport directly to market. First oil is expected before the end of 2017.

OCEAN TECHNOLOGY

Ocean technology is the fastest growing industry in the Newfoundland economy. The private sector has increased by 57% since 2001; total revenue has almost doubled, and private sector employment has increased by more than 65%. The combined value of the private and public ocean technology sector is just over a quarter of a billion dollars.

One of the most advanced offshore engineering basins in the world, at the **National Research Council-Institute for Ocean Technology**, is used to model offshore technologies and structures in wind, current, wave and ice conditions.

The **Flume Tank** at the **Marine Institute's Centre for Sustainable Aquatic Resources** is the only facility of its kind in North America and the largest in the world.

The **Ice Tank** at the **National Research Council-Institute for Ocean Technology** is the largest in the world with a usable ice sheet 76 m (250 ft) long.

Icebergs are a specialty at the **Marine Institute's Centre for Maritime Simulation.** The centre's Full Mission Ship Bridge Simulator models harsh weather environments, navigating in ice, operating in high sea states and iceberg management. The centre trains ships' officers in all situations.

NEWFOUNDLAND AND THE SEA

Whether through offshore oil exploration, the oil and gas sector, ocean technology, a non-traditional species fishery, aquaculture or a revival of the traditional cod fishery, the sea that surrounds Newfoundland will always be an integral part of the province's economy. The sea is at the very essence of the life of the province. This is vividly expressed in L. E. F. English's *Historic Newfoundland* with a quote by Lt. Col. William Wood, a prominent Canadian author and historian:

> "Newfoundland is an island of the sea if ever there was one. Nowhere else does the sea enter so intimately into the life of a people—calling, always calling them— loudly along a thousand miles of surf washed coastline, echoing up a hundred resounding fiords that search out the very heart of the land, whispering through a thousand little tickles—but calling, always calling its sons away to the fishing grounds and sometimes to the very seafaring ends of the earth."

Chapter eight

NEWFOUNDLAND MISCELLANEA

Many famous people have visited St. John's. **Captain Cook**, the Pacific explorer, mapped much of Newfoundland's coastline during the years 1763-1767. **Captain Bligh** of the *Bounty* visited the harbour during this period. **Marconi** sent his first wireless message across the Atlantic in 1901 from Signal Hill, using kites to keep his antennas aloft in the high winds.

John Alcock and **Arthur Brown** left St. John's from Lester's Field on Blackmarsh Road on June 14, 1919, and flew the first successful transatlantic flight to Clifden, County Galway, Ireland. The flight in the **Vickers-Vimy** took 16 hours and 12 minutes! A monument commemorating the flight stands on LeMarchant Road across from St. Clare's Hospital.

A **Vickers-Vimy replica** flew from St. John's and landed on Number Eight Fairway of the Connemara Golf Club near Clifden on July 3, 2005. The nonstop flight took 18 hours and 19 minutes. It was flown by Steve Fossett and Mark Rebholtz, honouring the first nonstop crossing of the Atlantic by Alcock and Brown.

Charles Lindberg flew through the Narrows on his solo flight to Paris in 1927.

Many **adventurers** have used St. John's as a starting and finishing place for their attempts to cross the Atlantic in hot air balloons, small craft, row boats, sailboats and aircraft.

Prominent people served with the U.S. forces at Fort Pepperrell. **John Williams** scored his first movie in St. John's, a tourist promotion for the Newfoundland government; actor/comedian **Bill Cosby** served at Argentia Naval Base and **The Four Aces**, a popular singing group in the 1950s, began their career in Newfoundland.

Replica Vickers-Vimy arriving in Clifden, Ireland, July 3, 2005
COURTESY DR. N. RUSTED

SOME OTHER INTERESTING NEWFOUNDLAND "FACTS" AND "FIRSTS"

❖ **Mistaken Point** on the southernmost tip of the Avalon Peninsula has some of the oldest and best-preserved fossils in the world, dated about 565 million years old.

❖ One of the most important inventions of World War I, the first version of the **gas mask**, was invented in Newfoundland in 1915 by Cluny MacPherson, a medical doctor.

❖ The **first smallpox vaccination** in North America was performed by Dr. John Clinch in Trinity in 1798. He was a friend and colleague of Dr. Edward Jenner, who discovered the smallpox vaccine in England.

❖ Newfoundland can still be considered a "**nursery for seamen**," as 30% of the Canadian Navy are Newfoundlanders and some fishermen provide crews for shipping in the offseason of the fishery.

❖ At the outbreak of World War II in 1939, 80 **German nationals, prisoners of war** were taken from ships at Botwood and placed in an internment camp constructed at Pleasantville in St. John's. They were transferred to western Canada in 1941.

❖ A battery-operated automatic **German weather station** was placed in a remote area of Labrador on October 23, 1943. It was not found until the 1980s. The U-boat's log reported that it transmitted data for only two weeks.

❖ Newfoundland was the British Empire's first colony and became the tenth province of Canada.

❖ **Labrador** became part of Newfoundland in 1763 after the Seven Years War.

❖ **First Newfoundland Legislature:** The home of the first legislature in Newfoundland was in a tavern on Kings Road owned by Mrs. Mary Travers. The Colonial Building was later built to house the legislature.

❖ **Backwards Seating Tradition of the Newfoundland House of Assembly:** John Garland, the first Speaker, started Newfoundland's backwards seating tradition (all other Commonwealth parliaments' Governments sit on the right in relation to the Speaker's seat) in the Kings Road tavern in 1833. John Garland wanted to sit next to the warm fire and so the Opposition had to sit on his right — on the other side of the fire. This Newfoundland House of Assembly tradition stands to this day.

❖ **Sealskin Seats in Newfoundland House of Assembly:** All the leather seats, desk blotters and coasters used by members of the Government and Opposition in the Newfoundland House of Assembly are made of sealskin. The government decided to visibly show support for the many practical uses of sealskin after worldwide Greenpeace protests resulted in the closure of the seal fishery.

- ❖ **St. John's sister city is Waterford, Ireland.** The government of Ireland gave St. John's a Waterford crystal vase in the shape of a whale tail inscribed in English and Gaelic with an Irish harp and cod fish. This vase can be viewed in the lobby of the Confederation Building.

- ❖ **North America's First New Year:** The people of St. John's are the first in North America to celebrate the New Year. St. John's is also the first to see the sun rise and set in North America.

ODDS AND ENDS

Crime and Punishment: The hanging of Eleanor Power, the first woman in North America is said to have occurred in St. John's in 1754. She and her husband murdered the local magistrate. She was hung and buried on the site of the Fortis Building on Water Street and Prescott Street.

The last woman hanged in Newfoundland was Catherine Snow. She is said to have been hanged from the second floor window of the old court house in 1834.

Barking Kettle was the name given to a large iron pot in which a mixture of spruce bark and water was boiled. Nets and sails were then immersed in the pot to get a protective coating for longer use in the elements.

Killick is the term used for an anchor made of wood and weighted with stones. A master seaman in the navy was referred to as a killick — perhaps due to his rank insignia of an anchor. To "dowse the killick" was the term used when throwing the anchor overboard.

A **Quintal** is a measure of fresh, dried or cured fish. It was traditionally measured "by eye," technically a hundredweight, but considered to be 112 lb (51 kg) to account for inexact calculation, differences in size and spoilage.

Outport is the name given to villages or small rural communities out of St. John's and the larger centres.

Fish Flakes: Built on poles near the shoreline, a fish flake is a platform usually made of poles covered with boughs and used to dry fish. They are described in the 1786 Logbook of HMS *Pegasus*: "Numerous supporters, exactly resembling Kentish hop poles, are first fixed in the ground; over these is placed a horizontal platform of similar poles; and the whole is finally overspread with a covering of dry fern. This sort of structure is called a Fish Flake by the fishermen."

Fishing Room: Land, stores, fishing flakes and other facilities in a cove or harbour from which the fishery is conducted, where the fish is landed and processed and the crew or family lived during the fishing season.

Newfoundland Dog: This large distinctive breed is thought to have evolved from dogs brought by Basques fishermen in the 1500s as ships' dogs, crossed with other dogs brought by the British. The Newfoundland is a strong working dog with a predominantly black, double coat of fur and webbed feet, and is a gentle good companion known for bravery and saving many from drowning. It was also used for carrying mail and first placed on a postage stamp in 1887. The pure-bred Newfoundland dog was saved from extinction by a local breeder, the Hon. Harold MacPherson, around the beginning of the 20th century when he established Westerland Kennels in St. John's.

The **Pitcher Plant** (*Sarracenia purpurea*) was declared the provincial flower of Newfoundland in 1954. The unusual plant, found mainly in bogs and marshes, has a large, single wine-red flower with a red and gold centre and pitcher-shaped leaves attached around the bottom of the stem. The hollow leaves fill with water and the insectivorous plant feeds from insects that become trapped inside. Queen Victoria chose the pitcher plant to be engraved on the new Newfoundland penny in the late 1800s.

The **Puffin** (*Fratercula arctica*), a small, pigeon-size bird noted for its colourful beak as well as its swimming and diving abilities, is

Newfoundland's provincial bird and can be found at the Witless Bay Ecological Reserve.

Seabirds: Some of the largest seabird colonies on earth are located in Newfoundland — kittiwakes, murres, gannets, razorbills, ospreys and hawks. Take a trip to Cape St. Mary's Ecological Reserve, one of the largest and most accessible seabird sanctuaries in North America. Newfoundland also has a large population of bald eagles.

Wildlife: Newfoundland is noted for its abundant wildlife. Moose are regularly seen along the highways where they are potentially dangerous for unwary motorists. From time to time they wander into the towns and cities. Bear, rabbit, beaver, fox and owl are also prevalent on the island. On the southern shore, south of St. John's, caribou were a common sight, particularly in the Avalon Wilderness Preserve. The population has dropped by almost two thirds and all hunting has been stopped in the Gray River area. Disease or predators, such as black bear, lynx and coyote, may be a reason for the decline. Many of Newfoundland's animals can be viewed at the Salmonier Nature Park, about 50 km (30 miles) from St. John's.

Newfoundland Flag: For many years Newfoundland used England's flag, the Union Jack, as its symbol, but the province wanted a flag that was distinctively its own in the 1970s. Premier Brian Peckford formed a committee in 1979, headed by Artist Christopher Pratt to select a design. The flag was officially described in 1980 by the selection committee as follows:

> "In this flag the primary colours of Red, Gold and Blue are placed against a background of white to allow the design to stand out clearly. White is representative of snow and ice; blue represents the sea; red represents human effort and gold our confidence in ourselves. The blue section, most reminiscent of the Union Jack, represents our commonwealth heritage which has so decisively shaped our present. The red and gold section, larger than the other, represents our future. The two

triangles outlined in red portray the mainland and island portions of our province reaching the way to what we believe will be a bright future … the whole flag represents our past, present and future."

The entire flag is one of symbolism — a Christian cross, Beothuk and Naskapi ornamentation, outline of the maple leaf in the centre, image of a trident to emphasize our continued dependence on the fishery and ocean resources. When hung as a banner, the arrow takes on the appearance of a sword to remind us of the sacrifice of our war veterans. The design of the flag takes us from our earliest Beothuk beginnings and points forward, representing our past, present and future.

Newfoundland Coat of Arms: The coat of arms was adopted by the Newfoundland Government on January 1, 1928.

The coat of arms was granted in 1637, but was unknown to authorities in Newfoundland until almost 300 years later.

The cross is based upon the cross of St. George, but of a different colour. The lions and unicorns are based upon those in the Arms of England, to which the unicorn had been added at the time of the union of England with Scotland.

The shield is surmounted by an elk and supported on either side by people representative of the now extinct Beothuk Indians of Newfoundland. The translation of the motto along the bottom is "Seek ye first the Kingdom of God."

Newfoundland Motto: "Quaerite Prime Regnum Dei." (Seek ye first the Kingdom of God.)

Nickname: Newfoundland is known affectionately as "The Rock."

Newfoundland Standard Time: Newfoundland time is 3 1/2 hours behind Greenwich Mean Time. It is the only place in North America to have a half hour time zone, one half hour later than Atlantic Time, dating from when it was part of the British Empire. An old joke says that "The world will end at midnight … 12:30 in Newfoundland!"

UNESCO World Heritage Sites: Gros Morne National Park, on the west coast, to recognize and preserve its unique geological landscape which has been described as the 8th Wonder of the World; and L'Anse aux Meadows, on the Northern Peninsula, as it shows the first evidence of European settlement in the New World at about 1000 AD, 500 years before the voyages of Columbus.

The Theory of Plate Tectonics Proven in Newfoundland: The area of Gros Morne National Park and the Tablelands in the Long Range Mountains on the Northern Peninsula is world renowned for its complex geology. It was here that geologists proved the theory of plate tectonics — continental drift.

St. Pierre & Miquelon: The two tiny islands off the south coast of Newfoundland are a Department of France. They are a piece of France in North America.

Historic Role in Communication & Travel: St. John's is closer to Europe than any other North American city, and closer to England than it is to Alberta — halfway across Canada. Thus Newfoundland has played an historic role in trans-atlantic communication and travel. Marconi received the first trans-atlantic wireless message and St. John's was the departure point for Alcock and Brown who made the first flight across the Atlantic. Heart's Content was the site of the first successful transatlantic cable, landed in 1866 by the ship *Great Eastern*. A major cable relay station was located in Heart's Content for over 100 years and brought many trained and educated people to the island.

Newfoundland Stamps: Newfoundland released about 300 different designs of postage stamps between 1857 and 1949 when Canadian stamps replaced Newfoundland stamps. Today, Newfoundland stamps and covers are collector's items and much sought after at auctions worldwide. One famous stamp issued by the

Newfoundland Government in 1932 remained in circulation until 1937 — its inscription, "Codfish Newfoundland Currency."

Newfoundland Currency: Newfoundland had its own currency, coinage and bank notes from 1834 to 1949 when it joined Confederation with Canada. They are now collector's items and only available from dealers.

The *Dictionary of Newfoundland English* by W. J. Kirwin, G. M. Story, and J. D. A. Widdowson is a guide to the verbal dialect and heritage of Newfoundland and Labrador. The dictionary gives pronunciations and explanations for "Newfoundland English."

Our Culture: Newfoundland has a rich culture of its own. Its songs, recitations and oral history are varied and plentiful. The unusual place names of our communities and natural landmarks are reminders of our forefathers' experiences, roots, imagination and sense of humour. The place names reflect the background of the French, Spanish, Portuguese, Basques, Irish, Scottish, and English.

Pronunciation of Newfoundland: Rhymes with understand, otherwise you will be marked as an "outsider" or CFA — "come from away."

Local food: Local dishes include lobster in season, cod tongues, fish and brewis (with or without scrunchions), seal meat, capelin, salmon, crab, mussels, rabbit, moose, flipper pie, toutons (fried bread dough), pea soup and Jigg's dinner — salt beef and cabbage with other vegetables and pease pudding — followed by Figgie Duff for afters. Dessert lovers find Newfoundland's berries to be delicious and distinctive. Partridgeberries, bake-apples and blueberries are the most popular fruit.

Newman's Port: The wine was traditionally shipped from Portugal as long ago as 1679 and stored in caves in the South-side Hills when it was discovered by accident that the wine had aged well in Newfoundland and taken on a new flavour. It was later aged in Newman Wine Vault's cellars built on the corner of Springdale and Water Streets in 1847. Newman's Port was aged at another location in St. John's from 1966 until 1998 and is now aged in its native Portugal. The wine vaults were purchased by the government and declared a Provincial Historic site in 1986. The building is on long-term lease to the Newfoundland Historic Trust and has been developed into an interpretive museum relating the long history of the liquor trade in Newfoundland. The building was given the Southcott Award for restoration in 1989.

Newman Wine Vaults
RUSTED COLLECTION

bibliography

Baker, Melvin. *The Government of St. John's, Newfoundland, 1800-1921.* Doctorate of Philosophy, Dept. of History, University of Western Ontario, London, Ontario, 1980.

Baker, Melvin and Graham, Jean. *Celebrate Memorial: A Pictorial History of Memorial University of Newfoundland.* St. John's: Memorial University Division of University Relations, 1999.

Baker, Melvin and Cando, James. "Signal Hill Gaol 1846-1859," *Newfoundland Quarterly* V.85 (4), 1990.

Barnes, Gordon (Manager) and Gerard Murphy (Collection Manager), Railway Coastal Museum, St John's. Interviews.

Briffett, Frances. *The Story of Newfoundland and Labrador.* Toronto: J.M. Dent and Sons (Canada) Limited, 1954.

Building On A Solid Base. Hibernia Management and Development Company Ltd., January 1995.

Cell, Gillian T. *English Enterprise in Newfoundland 1577-1660.* Toronto: University of Toronto Press, 1969.

Chadwick, St. John. *Newfoundland: Island into Province.* Cambridge: Cambridge University Press, 1967.

Charting a New Course Towards the Fishery of the Future. Report of the Task Force on Incomes and Adjustment in the Atlantic Fishery November 1993, Ottawa, Fisheries and Oceans Communications Directorate, 1993.

Cochrane Street Church. <www.cochranestreetuc.com/History.htm> Accessed Oct 2010.

Colonial Office Series 194. Colonial Office Original Correspondence. Board of Trade Newfoundland. London: Public Record Office.

Davies, Glanville J. *England and Newfoundland: Policy and Trade 1660-1783*. Doctorate of Philosophy, Dept. of History, University of Southampton, 1980.

East Coast Trail. <www.eastcoasttrail.ca>; <www.treksandtrailsinternational.com> Accessed Oct 2010.

The Economic Review 2009. Department of Finance, Government of Newfoundland and Labrador. November 23, 2009.

Encyclopaedia of Newfoundland and Labrador, Vol. 1, 1981; Vol. 2, 1984, 1st Editions, St. John's: Newfoundland Book Publishers (1967) Limited, Vol. 3, 1991; Vol. 4, 1993; Vol. 5, 1994; 1st Editions, St. John's: Harry Cuff Publications Limited.

English, L.E.F. *Historic Newfoundland*, Newfoundland Dept. of Tourism, 1974.

Graham, Gerald S. *Fisheries and Seapower*. Canadian Historical Association Annual Report. Ottawa: Canadian Historical Assoc. 1941.

The Grand Concourse – An Integrated Walkway System. Transport Canada. <www.tc.gc.ca/eng/programs/environment-utsp-grandconcourse> Accessed Sept 2010.

Greene, John P. *Trial and Triumph: The History of Newfoundland and Labrador*. Toronto: Doubleday Canada Limited, 1982.

Handcock, W. Gordon. *So Long as There Comes Noe Women: Origins of English Settlement in Newfoundland*. History Series 6. St. John's: Breakwater Books, 1989.

Harbour Survey — St. John's, Newfoundland. Parts I & II. Dept. of Public Works of Canada. Fenco, 1957.

Hebron Project Overview. Hebron Project Office, St John's, Newfoundland.

Heritage Canada. <www.heritagecanada.org/eng/services/awards> Accessed Sept 2010.

Heritage Buildings Report, Heritage Foundation of Newfoundland & Labrador. <www.heritagefoundation.ca> Accessed Oct 2010.

Hiller, James. "The Newfoundland Seal Fishery: An Historical Introduction," in *Bulletin of Canadian Studies*, V. 7 (2), 1983/4.

Hiller, James. "Newfoundland Confronts Canada, 1867 – 1949," Chapter 10 in *The Atlantic Provinces in Confederation*, E. R. Forbes and D. A. Muise, eds. Toronto: University of Toronto Press, 1993.

Historic Sites Association of Newfoundland & Labrador. The Manning Award. <www.historicsites.ca/manningaward> Accessed Nov 2010.

MacKay, R.A. *Newfoundland: Economic, Diplomatic and Strategic Studies.* Toronto: Oxford University Press, 1946.

MacLeod, Malcolm. *A Bridge Built Halfway: A History of Memorial University College, 1925-1950.* Montreal and Kingston: McGill-Queen's University Press, 1990.

McLintock, A. H. *The Establishment of Constitutional Government in Newfoundland 1783-1832.* Longman Green, 1941.

Matthews, Keith. *Lectures on the History of Newfoundland: 1500-1830.* St. John's: Breakwater Books, 1988.

Memorial University of Newfoundland. <www.mun.ca/> Accessed July 2010.

Moakley, L. D. *Ye Olde St. John's: Its Wells, Its Brooks, Its Unfamiliar Names.* Pamphlet. City of St John's Archives.

Mummers Troupe. <www.heritage.nf.ca/arts/mummerscollective> Accessed Jan 2011.

National Geographic. National Geographic Traveler Panel Rates 99 Coastal Destinations. <www.press.nationalgeographic.com/pressroom/> Accessed Nov 2010.

National Historic Sites. <www.pc.gc.ca/apps/> Accessed Oct 2010.

Newfoundland and Labrador. <www.newfoundlandlabrador.com> Accessed July 2010; <www.gov.nl.ca/> Accessed Nov 2010.

Newfoundland and Labrador's Registered Heritage Structures. <www.heritage.nf.ca/society/> Accessed Sept 2010.

Newfoundland Book of Remembrance. Memorial Reminders. <www.collections.mun.ca/Bookviewer/Remembrance> Accessed Nov 2010.

Newfoundland Historic Trust. <www.historictrust.com/> Accessed Oct 2010.

Newfoundland Royal Commission 1933 Report. London: His Majesty's Stationary Office, 1933.

Newfoundland Travelling Theatre Company. <www.heritage.nf.ca/arts/nttc> Accessed Dec 2010.

Newfoundland Symphony Orchestra. <www.nso-music.com/> Accessed Nov 2010.

Ocean Technology Excellence. Department of Trade and Innovation, Trade and Rural Development. Government of Newfoundland and Labrador, 2010.

Penney, Gerald Associates Limited. *South Castle Delineation Project - 1993*. Report of Excavations at Anchor Point, January 1995.

Penney, Gerald Associates Limited. *Under the Streets. Archeology and the Harbour Interceptor Sewer Project*. February 24, 2010.

Penney, Gerald. Rare Books and Maps of Newfoundland and Labrador. <Newfoundlandbooks.com>.

Plan Drafted for Dwindling Newfoundland Caribou. <www.cbc.ca/canada/newfoundlandlabrador/story/2008/02/08/caribou-study.html> Accessed Sept 2010.

Poynter, Adele, Executive Director, Johnson Geo Centre. Interview. <www.geocentre.ca> Accessed Aug 2010.

Prowse, D. W. *History of Newfoundland from English*, Colonial and Foreign Records. London: MacMillan and Co, 1985.

Pullen, Rear-Admiral H. F. *Atlantic Schooners*. Fredericton: Brunswick Press, 1967.

The Rooms Fast Facts. Information provided courtesy of The Rooms, St. John's.

Rose, George A. *Cod: The Ecological History of the North Atlantic Fishery*. St. John's: Breakwater Books, 2007.

Rowe, C. Francis. *In Fields Afar: A Review of the Establishment of the Anglican Parish of St. John's and Its Cathedral*. St. John's: Seawise Enterprises, 1989.

Rowe, Frederick W. *A History of Newfoundland and Labrador*. Toronto: McGraw-Hill Ryerson Limited, 1980.

Ryan, Shannon. *An Abstract of the C0194 Statistics*. Newfoundland Census Returns.

Smith, K. E. *St. John's: A National Harbours Board Project*. Filmstrip. MUN Clearinghouse, 1977.

Southcott Awards. <www.historictrust.ca/index.php/southcott-awards>.

St. John's Arts & Culture Centre History. <www.artsandculturecentre.com/stjohns/history> Accessed Sept 2010.

St John's Women: First and Last Hung in Newfoundland. <www.heritage.nf.ca/society/womenswalk> Accessed Jan 2011.

St. John's: A Harbour Reborn. Motion Picture, Ottawa. Crawley Films Ltd. Development and reconstruction of St. John's harbour, 1958-1963. The Newfoundland Archives (Donated by the Foundation of Canada Engineering Corporation Limited, St. John's.) <www.journals.sfu.ca/archivar>

The City of St John's. <www.stjohns.ca> Accessed Sept 2010.

Titanic. <Titanic.com> Accessed Aug 2010.

Whiteley, William. *James Cook in Newfoundland 1762-1767.* Newfoundland Historical Society. Pamphlet Number 3, 1975.

Young, Ewart, ed. *This is Newfoundland.* Toronto: Ryerson Press, 1949.

Welcome to Hibernia. <www.hibernia.ca/> Accessed July 2010.

Wesley United Church. <http://www.wesleychurch.ca/> Accessed Oct 2010.

acknowledgements

Many thanks go to the following people for their help and encouragement in this project:

Heather Mills Snow, Economic Development and Tourism, City of St. John's; Helen Miller, Archivist, St. John's City Archives; Gerry Penney, Gerald Penney Associates Limited; Tim Murphy, Marketing, Chevron Canada; Brian Smart, Vice President Operations, and Bob McCarthy, Director Business Development, St. John's Port Authority; Dr. George Rose, Director, Centre for Fisheries Ecosystem Research, Fisheries and Marine Institute; Derek Butler, Newfoundland and Labrador Seafood Producers; Fisheries and Oceans, Canada Research; Mark Dolomount, Executive Director, Professional Fish Harvesters Certification Board; Captain Dr. Jim Parsons, Marine Institute.

Bob Halfyard, Operations Manager, Pippy Park; Chrysta Collins, Communications Officer, and Sandra Ronayne, Archivist at The Rooms; Gordon Barnes and Gerard Murphy, Railway Coastal Museum; Greg Keating, Manager GIS Engineering Dept., City of St. John's; Elizabeth Gallagher, Sergeant at Arms, Confederation Building; Dan Hyde, Memorial University; Adele Poynter, Executive Director, GEO Centre; Andy Jones, Andy Jones Productions; Margo Bruce O'Connell and Sheila Anstey, ExxonMobil; Trevor Bennett, Information Resources Manager, Sheila Downey and Amanda Oakley, Canada-Newfoundland and Labrador Offshore Petroleum Board

(CNLOPB); Reginald Winsor, Executive Director, Newfound-
land and Labrador Arts Council; Neachel Keeping, St. John's
City Archives; Amy House, Artistic Animateur, and Suzanne
Mullett, General Manager, Resource Centre for the Arts LSPU
Hall; Francesca Swann; Ian Knight, Geologist; Bill Rompkey;
Bob Piercey, Fluvarium; Claire Jenkins; Larry and Brenda
Parsons; Kevin Gushue, Tourism Manager, and Donna Bishop,
Tourism Information Councilor, City of St. John's; Ann
Schofield, Leoframes Antique Prints in Brighton England;
Gemma Giovannini; Dr. Jim Hiller and Dr. Shannon Ryan
for inspiring me to learn more about Newfoundland history;
my father Dr. Nigel Rusted for the use of his library and
photographs. Special thanks to my editor Annamarie Beckel;
Rhonda Molloy; Joan Ritcey, Centre for Newfoundland
Studies, MUN; and Dr. Arthur May.

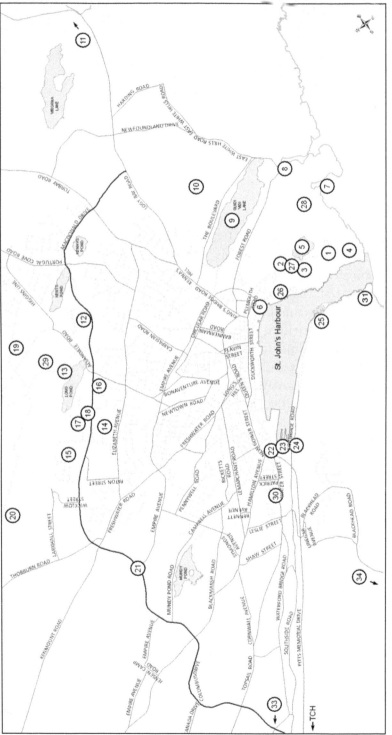

St. John's – The New Extended City
CITY OF ST. JOHN'S

◀